FLESH AND BLOOD

FLESH AND BLOOD

ADOLESCENT GENDER DIVERSITY AND VIOLENCE

James W. Messerschmidt

Rowman & Littlefield Publishers, Inc.
Lanham • Boulder • New York • Toronto • Oxford

ROWMAN & LITTLEFIELD PUBLISHERS, INC.

Published in the United States of America
by Rowman & Littlefield Publishers, Inc.
A wholly owned subsidiary of The Rowman & Littlefield Publishing Group, Inc.
4501 Forbes Boulevard, Suite 200, Lanham, Maryland 20706
www.rowmanlittlefield.com

PO Box 317, Oxford OX2 9RU, UK

British Library Cataloguing in Publication Information Available

Library of Congress Cataloging-in-Publication Data
Messerschmidt, James W.
    Flesh and blood : adolescent gender diversity and violence / James W. Messerschmidt.
        p.   cm.
    Includes bibliographical references and index.
    ISBN 0-7425-4163-0 (cloth : alk. paper) — ISBN 0-7425-4164-9 (pbk. :alk. paper)
    1. Youth and violence—Sex differences. 2. Violence in adolescence—Sex differences.
3. Identity (Psychology) in youth. 4. Sex differences (Psychology) 5. Crime—
Sociological aspects. I. Title: Adolescent gender diversity and violence. II. Title.

HQ799.2.V56M47 2004
303.6'0835—dc22

2004011763

Printed in the United States of America

∞™ The paper used in this publication meets the minimum requirements of American
National Standard for Information Sciences—Permanence of Paper for Printed Library
Materials, ANSI/NISO Z39.48–1992.

For my loving flesh and blood, Ulla, Erik, and Jan

CONTENTS

CONTENTS

FOREWORD

In the last few decades, the link between our society's gender arrangements and our patterns of violence, criminality, and punishment has become a closely studied question. As everyone knows, most killers are men, most batterers are men, most prisoners are men, and most soldiers, guerrillas, police officers, and jailers are men. But most men are not violent.

Why is this so? Mass media and conservative politicians still tell us this is a matter of "natural" difference and that raging hormones need to be brought under control, preferably with a sharp jolt of imprisonment. But serious investigators know the question involves much more than that. James Messerschmidt's first achievement in this book is to give us a vivid history of criminological thought on this subject. He traces, for instance, the deep confusions in ideas about gender, and the dramatic reversals of criminologists' ideas about the role of the body in generating criminal behavior.

We now know that our society's systems of social control themselves construct gender differences. Women, generally speaking, are subject to a different pattern of social policing from men, principally directed at their appearance, decorum, and sexuality rather than their violence. Issues about crime and control are not marginal to gender—they are, in fact, deeply interwoven with the gender system.

We also know that gender is not passively suffered, but actively made. We have become aware that crime or transgression can be a significant resource in the making of masculinity and femininity. We know that violence is to a large extent a product of institutions and their functioning, and that institutions themselves embed and propagate gender patterns.

James Messerschmidt has been a major figure in the growth of this new understanding. He has developed the most coherent and sophisticated conceptual analysis of the link between masculinities and crime. He has also conducted superb close-focus empirical investigations, particularly with young people, which reveal in exceptional detail the gender dynamics in specific patterns of offending.

In this book, James Messerschmidt moves our understanding forward again. He addresses the problem of how the body is caught up in social processes—a major issue in gender studies. It isn't that the body is a blank page on which society writes; the body is "lived," as Messerschmidt argues, is central to experience, and is an active player in the social process. In this book we move a long way from stereotyped ideas of biological determinism. Yet we still see how bodies, their growth, and people's hopes, fears, and experiences about their bodies play an active role in the making of gendered violence.

The book also deals, in an insightful and sympathetic way, with the contradictions and ambiguities of gender. It is possible for women to "do masculinity" and for men to "do femininity." In this book, in fascinating case studies, we are given a pioneering account of how these complexities in gender play out in the production of violence. The book has wide significance for gender studies, a field in which these problems have become important. It suggests ways of moving beyond binaries of sex versus gender, body versus mind, and, of course, the simple gender binary itself. It also draws attention to the way gender practices vary between settings. The same person may enact gender differently in the home, the school, and the street.

It is rare for new conceptual thinking to be closely connected to powerful empirical research. That connection has been James Messerschmidt's trademark, and in this book, by this means, he opens up fresh perspectives on issues we desperately need to understand—youth, bodies, gender, and violence. I am pleased to introduce this exceptional work. I am sure that all readers, whether familiar with criminology or not, will learn a great deal from it.

R. W. Connell, University of Sydney

ACKNOWLEDGMENTS

I am forever deeply grateful to Lenny, Perry, Tina, and Kelly for talking openly with me and sharing their lives—they comprise the core of this book. Without the cooperation of these four youths, as well as their parents and guardians, this book would have never been written.

I am particularly indebted to Bob Connell, who as a friend and mentor devoted much time and energy to this book in reading the entire manuscript and contributing very important comments, criticisms, and a wonderful foreword. Numerous people also read drafts of the manuscript—in whole or in part—at various stages of its development, and contributed greatly to the editorial process: Kathy Davis, Sarah Fenstermaker, Nancy Jurik, Willem de Haan, Bob Miller, Brigitte Scott, Christine Williams, Val Jenness, Jill McCorkel, Dana Britton, and Jody Miller. I thank all of these people for sharing their thoughts and ideas. Finally, Lauren Webster was a superb research assistant for this project, and the students in my graduate seminars on gender and crime at the University of Stockholm, Sweden, advanced keen insight toward improving my methodology and theoretical perspective.

Access to the boys and girls interviewed for this project was made possible by a number of people who graciously took time away from their own work to help me. Special thanks to the University of Southern Maine's Institutional Review Board, particularly the associate provost and dean of graduate studies Margo Wood for her wonderful help with the consent form, as well as several people who work with violent youth: Sheila McKinley, Daniel Nee, and Tina Vermiglio. I also thank the interim dean of the College of Arts and Sciences, Luisa Deprez, and Provost Joe Wood—both at the University of Southern Maine—for supporting my work by awarding me an important sabbatical.

As always, the Access and Interlibrary Loan Services librarians at the University of Southern Maine's Glickman Family Library have been an essential component to my research. I thank in particular Cassandra Fitzherbert and David Vardeman for their crucial assistance.

I owe considerable thanks to Rowman & Littlefield publisher Jon Sisk for his continued interest in and support of my work. I also wish to extend much appreciation to the entire Rowman & Littlefield staff, but especially to Alan McClare, executive editor, and Kärstin Painter, associate editor.

Most of all I thank my own flesh and blood—to whom this book is dedicated—for not simply their love and encouragement, but for their contributions to this book by consistently challenging my conceptualizations: Ulla solidly sharpened my thinking on "girls doing masculinity"; Jan profoundly impacted my thoughts on the mind–body binary; and Erik intensely moved me to rethink what constitutes "art"—what a wonderful family I have!

PART I

ANATOMY OF A DISCIPLINE

• 1 •

CORPOREAL CRIMINOLOGY

If one empirical observation is unquestionable, it is that the vast majority of those who engage in crime do so with, and through, their bodies. Whenever individuals engage in the harms sociological criminologists label crime—from street to suite—they often use and rely on their bodies to carry out such acts. Despite this primacy of the body to crime, however, sociological criminologists historically have eschewed an examination of how the body actually relates to crime. This exclusion of the body from sociological criminology is rooted partially in a rejection of nineteenth- and early twentieth-century biological and multifactor perspectives. Sociological criminology emerged by exclusively embracing the social causes of crime as the principal object of theoretical focus—emphasis on the social provided a secure defense against attempts to explain crime as simply epiphenomena of biology. Thus, sociological criminologists adopted a disembodied approach to crime that was distinct from and irreducible to biology. In proclaiming criminology as exclusively a sociological discipline—as, for example, Edwin Sutherland did in the late 1920s and early 1930s (Laub and Sampson 1991)—sociological criminologists historically left to biology the task of scrutinizing the body. Accordingly, in sociological criminology the body—biologically or phenomenologically—was denied any place in the formation of self and crime. Let's look closer at this development and how it is related to gender.

BECCARIA, BENTHAM, AND THE BODY

Michael Foucault reports in *Discipline and Punish* (1979) that during the late sixteenth, seventeenth, and eighteenth centuries the most serious crimes in Europe were punished in a public ceremony wherein the body of the accused was ritually tortured and dismembered. A telling account of such an execution is his synopsis of the death of regicide Robert Francois Damiens, who was tortured in a most horrific manner—his body drawn and quartered by horses tied to each arm and each leg. Accordingly, the penalty was imprinted onto his body in detail for the entire community to observe, the public nature of the corporeal punishment used to signal the sovereign power of the king. Because all crimes were considered offenses against the king, the body of the condemned became "a screen upon which sovereign power is projected, or, more precisely, a flesh upon which the marks of power can be visibly engraved" (Garland 1990, 140).

Enlightenment scholars opposed this form of bodily punishment because of its harsh, capricious, and inhumane nature. Cesare Beccaria (1764), for example, declared that punishment must not be cruel and simply the mercurial personal decision of a judge. He advocated instead that "the punishment should fit the crime" and incarceration should be employed as the standard form of penalty in order to prevent "free-willed" people from violating the law.[1] Moreover, Jeremy Bentham (1780) suggested that a special type of prison, the panopticon, be constructed: a three-storied circular building in which individual isolated cells around the perimeter would be under constant observation from the inspector's lodge—a central tower located in the middle of the prison. The operative principles of the panopticon were isolation and perpetual surveillance. And the effect of this surveillance was "to induce in the inmate a state of conscious and permanent visibility that assures the automatic functioning of power" (Foucault 1979, 201). The beneficial effects of this type of prison were stated by Bentham in 1787: "Morals reformed—health preserved—industry invigorated—instruction diffused—public burdens lightened—economy seated, as it were, upon a rock—all by the simple idea of architecture" (cited in Bowring 1962, 39).

As Foucault (1979) points out, panopticism became the central metaphor for modern disciplinary power based on isolation, individuation, and supervision. Indeed, Beccaria's ideas were included in the French Code of 1791, and Bentham's conception of the disciplinary prison grew to become widely accepted throughout Europe and the United States (Beirne 1993). For Foucault, then, the focus in Western societies changes during this time period, evidenced by the transformed nature of punishment: In contrast to public torture and execution of the "body" in the sixteenth through the eighteenth centuries, punishment in the nineteenth century demanded bodies be locked away in a controlled institution to permit manipulation of the "mind." Under the constant scrutiny of prison authorities and regulated according to a strict timetable, prisoner bodies thus were socially constructed through their subjection to discipline and reformation. In other words, the prison developed as a "disciplinary institution" that fashioned techniques for organizing and training inmates into bodily "normalcy." By the mid-nineteenth century, Foucault argues, Western societies became essentially disciplinary societies where more and more people were placed in organizations—school, clinic, asylum, prison—whose goal was to create a body of "normals" for adequate participation in the marketplace. Panopticism resonates throughout Western societies so that "prisons resemble factories, schools, barracks, hospitals, which all resemble prisons" (1979, 228). Beccaria and Bentham—and therefore "classical criminology"—emerged from their opposition to torture of the body and their embeddedness in the "machinery that assumes responsibility for and places under surveillance" the "mind" (1979, 77).[2]

"SCIENTIFIC" CRIMINOLOGY AND CORPOREAL DIFFERENCE

Despite this emphasis on the alleged benefits of the panopticon, the collection of "social statistics" on the rising rates of crime and recidivism in the 1800s showed that the new penal strategies of Beccaria and Bentham had failed to reform the "mind" and that this defeat was an essential condition for the application of new statistical techniques to the causes of crime (Beirne 1993). Adolphe Quetelet (1796–1874)—among the first of his time to examine the French crime statistics published in the 1800s—showed that crime was surprisingly regular in society, that it remained fairly constant over time, and that individual types of crime remained about the same proportion of the total over time (Beirne 1993).

During the 1840s, Quetelet drew on the "sciences" of physiognomy and phrenology, which had gained widespread prestige throughout much of Europe and the United States by the mid-nineteenth century. Both sciences purported to find signs of inner character on the surface of the body, particularly on the head and face (Sekula 1986). Indeed, it was Quetelet who first suggested a relationship between the body and crime, assigning "phrenological defects a causal role in the genesis of crime" (Beirne 1993, 90). Quetelet argued that individuals with phrenological defects had high criminal propensities, but that such tendencies could be modified by the particular social milieu in which an individual was embedded. In his 1871 book *Anthropometrie*, Quetelet made use of anthropometry measurements, and as Beirne shows, he "explicitly juxtaposed crime rates and the proportions of the human body as instances of complementary social facts. Both varied by age, sex, and race, and obeyed the same law-like conditions" (1993, 90).

Quetelet, then, was the first to identify the *body* as being somehow related to "deviance" ("criminal man" possessed corporeal deviations from what Quetelet labeled "average man"), and his work represented the beginning of a major shift in the conceptualization of crime, now reconfigured as a "social problem"—a patterned and undesirable consequence of social life rather than simply individual acts threatening the sovereignty of the king (Horn 2003). Thus, "positivists" like Quetelet perceived society as threatened by the *criminal body*, and the body of the criminal was conceived as a sign of social dangerousness and deviation from the statistical norm (Horn 2003, 12).

It was anthropometry, then, that first promised to make known the alleged "dangers" to society by uncovering *the* "criminal body." Cesare Lombroso (1835–1909) was the preeminent nineteenth-century criminologist to employ this method. In his book *Criminal Man* (1876), Lombroso claimed that many of the bodily characteristics found in "savages and among the colored races are also to be found in habitual delinquents" (cited in Beirne 1993, 149). For Lombroso, the criminal body—with its atavistic stigmata—represented an evolutionary reversion that was driven biologically to act as *normal* savages would. Lombroso argued that he had uncovered a distinct human type who commits crime, a *corporeal difference* between criminals and noncriminals, and the existence of a "male born criminal." Thus, Lombroso—as the founder of the new science of criminal anthropology—defined the body, especially the head and face, as the signature of social dangerousness. Notwithstanding, Lombroso and his followers "scientifically" read the bodies of "criminals" to differentiate men and women as well as criminal and noncriminal.

In *Criminal Woman, the Prostitute, and the Normal Woman*,[3] Lombroso and Gugliemo Ferrero argued that female born criminals maintain "criminal propensities" that "are more intense than even those of their male counterparts." As Lombroso and Ferrero went on to point out, "[T]he female born criminal surpasses her male counterpart in the refined, diabolic cruelty with which she commits her crimes. Merely killing her enemy does not satisfy her; she needs to watch him suffer and experience the full taste of death" (1893, 182).

The female born criminal is similar to "normal women" and children in being "deficient in the moral sense . . . vengeful, jealous, and inclined to refined cruelty when . . . [taking] revenge." Indeed, for Lombroso and Ferrero, the criminal woman and the noncriminal woman are similar in being "big children" whose "evil tendencies are more numerous and varied than men's, but usually . . . remain latent. When awakened and excited, however, these evil tendencies lead to proportionately worse results" (1893, 183). In short, the born female criminal is "doubly exceptional, first as a woman and then as a criminal. This is because criminals are exceptions among civilized people, and women are exceptions among criminals. . . . As a double exception, then, the criminal woman is a true monster" (1893, 183–185). According to Lombroso the born female criminal was more atavistic than the normal woman, but all women—whether criminal or not—had yet to evolve as far as white men. For Lombroso, women simply were more corporeal than men.

Lombroso thus ushered in the new science of criminology by focusing on the "visible body" as allegedly demarcating a *corporeal difference* between criminal and noncriminal as well as between men and women. In other words, criminology was gendered from its beginning, as the origin of "scientific criminology" rested on claims alleging an inferior corporeal difference between men and women. And of course Lombroso and Ferrero were not alone in this belief inasmuch as even their staunchest contemporary critics agreed that women were biologically inferior to men. For example, Gabriel Tarde (1843–1904) argued that women have less "voluminous crania and brains that are less heavy" than men's (and thus women were less intelligent than men) and that improvidence, vanity, a lack of inventiveness, and a tendency to imitate others are all inherent in, and shared by, women and criminals (cited in Horn 2003, 53, 166).

MAKING "SEX"

It is important to understand criminology's emphasis on corporeal difference in context—Lombroso and his colleagues were not objective scientists, but brought to their work on crime a specific conception of "sex" difference, and proceeded then to discern bodily "facts" and construct theoretical "explanations" consistent with their beliefs. Their scientific work was grounded in a specific cultural framework that viewed "sex" strictly as dichotomous and unchanging. In other words, the earliest "scientific" criminologists began with the assumption that there are but two "natural" sexes, and then proceeded to find bodily evidence supporting that assumption.

Historical research, however, problematizes the notion of a "natural" unchanging "sex" dichotomy; Thomas Laqueur's (1990) work is seminal in this regard. Laqueur shows that for two thousand years a "one-sex model" dominated scientific and popular thought in which male and female bodies were not conceptualized in terms of difference. From antiquity to the late 1600s, male and female bodies were seen as fundamentally similar, even in terms of genitalia, with the vagina regarded as an interior penis, the vulva as foreskin, the uterus as scrotum, and the ovaries as testicles. Although women were considered inferior to men, their bodies were not a different "sex," and did not inhere that inferiority in any fixed way. As Laqueur pointed out, "*Sex*, or the body, must be understood as the epiphenomenon, while *gender*, what we would take to be a cultural category, was primary or 'real'" (1990, 8). Gender inequality was imposed on bodies from the *outside*, not from the *inside*. To be a man or a woman from antiquity to the late seventeenth century was to hold a social rank, to have a specific place in society, "not to *be* organically one or the other of two incommensurable sexes. Sex before the seventeenth century, in other words, was still a sociological and not an ontological category" (Laqueur 1990, 8). The shift in thinking to a "two-sex model"—consisting of two different types of human and sexual natures, "male" and "female" (for example, the "essence" of femininity was now found in the ovaries)—corresponded to the emergence of the public/private split: It was now "natural" for men to enter the public realm of society and it was "natural" for women to remain in the private sphere. Explaining these distinct gendered spaces was "resolved by grounding social and cultural differentiation of the sexes in a biology of incommensurability" (Laqueur 1990, 19). In other words, "gender" became subordinated to "sex" and biology was considered primary: *the* foundation of gender inequality in society.

Laqueur makes clear that the change to a two-sex model was not the result of advances in science, inasmuch as the reevaluation of the body as primary occurred approximately one hundred years before alleged supporting scientific discoveries appeared (1990, 9). Indeed, and although anatomical and physiological differences clearly exist between male and female bodies, what counted as "sex" was determined socially:

> To be sure, difference and sameness, more or less recondite, are everywhere; but which ones count and for what ends is determined outside the bounds of empirical investigation. The fact that at one time the dominant discourse construed the male and female bodies as hierarchically, vertically, ordered versions of one sex and at another time as horizontally ordered opposites, as incommensurable, must depend on something other than even a great constellation of real or supposed discoveries. (Laqueur 1990, 10)

In short, natural scientists had no interest in "seeing" two distinct sexes, at the anatomical and concrete physiological level, "until such differences became politically important" and "sex" therefore became "explicable only within the context of battles over gender and power" (Laqueur 1990, 10, 11).

Such a gendered battle existed in Italy when Lombroso was making his "scientific" discoveries. As Nicole Hahn Rafter and Mary Gibson (2004, 16) point out in their introduction to *Criminal Woman*:

It is not coincidental that *Criminal Woman* was published during a period when members of the women's movement were vociferously demanding access to education, entrance to the professions, equality within the family, and the right to vote. . . . [T]he prospect of a fundamental restructuring of gender roles deeply, and perhaps unconsciously, troubled him [Lombroso] as his allocation of the first major section of *Criminal Woman* to proofs of the inferiority of normal women shows. His ridicule of intellectual women and his insistence on maternity as the proper aspiration for all women scientifically affirmed traditional stereotypes and directly challenged the vision of female emancipationists.

Rafter and Gibson continue to argue that Lombroso's work:

> presented an enormous problem for the nascent Italian women's movement, which saw science as a potential ally in the struggle against the restrictive gender roles endorsed by religious and conservative thinkers. With the publication of *La donna delinquente*, however, supporters of women's rights were instead faced with a book purporting to present modern empirical proof of women's inferiority. . . . *Criminal Woman* weakened the Italian women's movement in its quest for expanded legal and political rights for women. (2004, 18)

In short, certain corporeal criteria were "seen" historically and socially by Lombroso and many of his contemporaries in a way that buttressed the unequal sex dichotomy. Lombroso did not discover corporeal difference but, rather, came to know the body *through gender*. The emergence of criminology as a "scientific" discipline was based on alleged corporeal "sex" differences that had been articulated within already existing gender power relations.

SOCIAL MAN, CORPOREAL WOMAN

Though sociology as an academic discipline developed in France, the United States, Britain, and Germany in the final two decades of the nineteenth century, it nevertheless flourished primarily in the United States between 1920 and 1950 (Connell 1997b). The focus of sociological knowledge during this time was on internal "social problems" of U.S. society, marked by "the prominence of the Chicago school's urban research and the growth of specializations within sociology" (Connell 1997b, 1536). One such specialization was, of course, criminology.

Edwin Sutherland (1924) published the first sociological textbook on crime, which was intended as a review of the current literature on the causes of crime and on the social control of crime. In his book *Criminology*, Sutherland presented an eclectic multifactor perspective in which he noted that a combination of biological and social conditions affected crime (1924, 179–182). However, a mere two years after the publication of his first edition, Sutherland rejected biology as an essential component for understanding crime and introduced a perspective that concentrated exclusively on the social. In "The Biological and Sociological Processes," Sutherland (1926, 60) argued that sociological processes are unique and differ from biological processes in that a social act must always be a joint act in which other individuals participate in some way, "and the act of each individual must appear in the act of the other participants." In sociological processes, "[o]ne takes the part of, puts himself [sic] in the place of, or plays the role of, these others" (1926, 60). For Sutherland, the essential characteristic of social processes was social interaction in which the act of each person had meaning to the other person: "Meaning is an objective thing, inhering in the behavior of the participants and in the objects with reference to which they act" (1926, 60).

Sutherland (1926, 62) pointed out that many sociologists of his time attempted to explain sociological processes by relating them to "the entire universe outside those processes" (such as a combination of sociological, biological, and psychological processes). However, Sutherland now argued against multifactor or "synthetic methods" (as he called them) inasmuch as numerous studies had shown that what earlier had been explained in terms of biological factors could now be articulated more satisfactorily in terms of social interaction: "Thus, at one time crime was explained as due to biological equipment. Now it is rather generally agreed by sociologists that we have practically no explanation of crime in terms of biology" (1926, 62). Sutherland maintained that sociology should separate from other disciplines—such as biology—so that a sociology of crime could be effected scientifically: "The most significant reason for the separation of sociology from biology is that it makes possible a limitation of the task of the sociologist so that his [sic] task can be performed scientifically. No science can deal with the entire universe. Nor can any science explain all concatenations of particular events" (1926, 64).

John Laub and Robert Sampson (1991, 1420) pointed out that during this period Sutherland was developing a form of sociological positivism in which crime was viewed "as a social phenomenon that could *only* be explained by social (i.e., nonindividual) factors." This is not surprising, as Sutherland was influenced greatly by such members of the Chicago School of Sociology as Robert Park, Ernest Burgess, Louis Wirth, and George Herbert Mead, as well as by Frederick Thrasher's (1927) sociological research on gangs and Clifford Shaw and Henry McKay's (1929) early work on the geographic distribution of delinquency (Gaylord and Galliher 1988). The result was that Sutherland accepted the idea that crime should be conceptualized exclusively "from the point of view of its relation to the social situation in which it occurs" (1926, 89). Sutherland found in the work of Charles Horton Cooley the theoretical tools necessary to forgo biology and construct a sociological perspective that concentrated on social interaction in particular social situations. For example, in "Social Process in Behavior Problems" Sutherland (1932, 113) utilized Cooley's position on social process, concluding:

> The social process by which delinquent behavior develops is the same as the social process by which non-delinquent behavior develops. . . . The variant is not in the social process but in the situation. Consequently social process may be a valuable step in the explanation of delinquent behavior, but it does not in itself contain the explanation of delinquent behavior as contrasted with non-delinquent behavior, since the process is the same in each.

Sutherland's interaction and interviews with a professional thief—eventually published in book form in 1937 as *The Professional Thief*—primarily taught him what it was that conveyed criminality through social process. As he put it: "I had worked for several years with a professional thief and had been greatly impressed by his statement that a person cannot become a professional thief merely by wanting to be one; he must be trained in personal association with those who are already professional thieves" (1956, 17).

Consequently, by the end of the 1930s Sutherland (1956, 19) had concluded that "learning, interaction, and communication were the processes around which a theory of criminal behavior should be developed. The theory of differential association was an attempt to explain criminal behavior in that manner." Indeed, in the 1939 edition of his textbook, Sutherland (4–5) proposed that "systematic criminal behavior is determined in a process of association with those who commit crimes, just as systematic lawful behavior is determined in a process of association with those who are law-abiding," and it is this "differential association" that "is the specific causal process in the development of systematic criminal behavior."

Sutherland bolstered his view that biology has nothing to do directly with criminality by attacking vehemently multifactor approaches that included a biological dimension in their analyses. For example, in their examination of the 1930s debate between Sutherland and Sheldon and Eleanor Glueck, Laub and Sampson conclude that Sutherland's adherence exclusively to a social explanation

> resulted in a theory that virtually required him to destroy individual-level, or nonsociological, perspectives on crime. The Gluecks advocated a multi-factor theory of crime, which to Sutherland represented a threat to the intellectual status

of sociological criminology. Hence, Sutherland's attack was aimed largely at extinguishing their interdisciplinary model so that sociology could establish proprietary rights to criminology.

Laub and Sampson argue further that "Sutherland became the warrior for sociology's coup of criminology" and viewed rejection of individual factor perspectives (biological, psychological, and multifactor) "as a 'professional turf' concern in making the case for a sociological criminology with himself as its leader" (1991, 1421).[4] Indeed, in their detailed treatment of the emergence and development of differential association theory, Mark Gaylord and John Galliher (1988, 137) argue that Sutherland "was quick to jump to sociology's defense whenever he perceived a threat from outsiders. As a master of critical and searching analysis he fulfilled the role of vigilant guardian superbly. As a result he won the unflagging support of his colleagues." Not surprisingly, Sutherland was elected president of the American Sociological Association in 1939.

In Sutherland's final version of differential association theory he presented a perspective that maintained a strict dichotomy between the social and the biological, focusing on the former as defining exclusively the realm of criminological inquiry. In the fourth edition of his textbook published in 1947 (three years before his death), Sutherland listed nine steps in "the process by which a particular person comes to engage in criminal behavior"—establishing crime as a "learned" behavior through interaction with others in intimate personal group settings, and the learning included the techniques of committing crime as well as the motives, drives, rationalizations, and attitudes necessary to engage in crime (Sutherland 1947, 6–7).

The exclusion of the body from sociological criminology thus is found partially in the epistemological foundations of differential association theory that are rooted in a rejection of nineteenth- and early twentieth-century biological and multifactor perspectives. Sociological criminology emerged by embracing social interaction and the learning of definitions favorable to lawbreaking as the principal objects of theoretical focus. As Sutherland implicitly claimed, as early as 1926, social interaction and the learning of crime need never be reduced to biology; the emphasis on the social provided a secure challenge against attempts to explain crime simply as epiphenomena of biology. Although clearly an important breakthrough in the history of sociological criminology, Sutherland nevertheless adopted a *disembodied* approach to crime. In proclaiming criminology exclusively a sociological discipline, then, Sutherland followed the dichotomization of culture and nature—and the Cartesian mind–body split—that developed in sociology generally during this time period (Turner 1996). The focus of sociological criminology was examination of social and cultural processes affecting the mind; it was left to biology to scrutinize the body.[5]

Moreover, this emphasis by Sutherland on the social was, from its beginning, gendered. Sutherland's concentration clearly was on boys, men, and crime, as he all but ignored girls, women, and crime. In his textbook, women are omitted altogether and girls are discussed solely in terms of their conformity. For example, in a section on the "sex ratio of crime," girls are depicted by Sutherland as identical— *all* girls "from infancy" are "taught that they must be nice" and, therefore, they commit very little crime relative to boys (1947, 101). This is the extent of Sutherland's discussion of girls and women. Arguably, Ngaire Naffine (1987, 31) is correct when she states that for Sutherland—as for the vast majority of criminologists during and after him—"Femaleness emerges as an anomaly."

This anomalous conception of girls and women is found also in his critique of the Gluecks's work noted earlier, where Sutherland completely ignored *Five Hundred Delinquent Women* (1934) (a book by the Gluecks that was their sole work on women and girls), which vividly argued that women's "special" biological (as well as social and economic) condition created "a soil so unfavourable we can scarcely expect a hardy fruit" (Glueck and Glueck 1934, 73). Thus, Sutherland (not unlike other sociologists of his time) dislodged boys and men—but not girls and women—from the realm of the corporeal and placed them squarely in the realm of the social. As Anne Witz and Barbara Marshall (2003, 351) put it, an ontology of *difference* was evoked that rendered "man as social and society as male."

As I have documented in greater detail elsewhere (Messerschmidt 1993), continuing to the early 1970s the history of sociological criminology is for the most part a history of research and theories written *by men* and about *social man* (although not *gendered man*). And although sociological criminologists recurrently disregarded women, when women were finally acknowledged the emphasis in sociological criminology on *social man* occurred alongside an emphasis on *corporeal woman*. Indeed, Lombroso's *Criminal Woman* was *the* major influence on conceptions of women and crime from the late 1800s until the early 1970s, primarily because so few sociological criminologists were willing to challenge that perspective (Rafter and Gibson 2004). A prime example that followed in the footsteps of Lombroso, the Gluecks, and others is the work of Otto Pollak who published *The Criminality of Women* in 1950 and who cited favorably Lombroso's conclusions as well as passionately supporting his combined "quantitative and qualitative approach." As a multifactor sociological criminologist—like the Gluecks—Pollak did acknowledge the influence on women of some social conditions, and he did discuss a few inequalities between men and women as impacting women's involvement in crime. Nevertheless, Pollak's (1950, 5) major argument was that although women's crime most likely equaled that of men's, women's crime was largely "masked criminality." This was so for several reasons that located the *primary* cause of women's crime *in* the female body.

First, Pollak argued that women were "addicted" to crimes that were concealed easily, such as shoplifting, prostitute theft, domestic theft, abortion, and perjury. Consequently, the crimes committed by women were more often underreported. Second, women were biologically more deceitful than men and, therefore, more prone to criminal concealment. Pollak stated that this "natural" deceit derived from the biological fact that a man "must achieve an erection in order to perform the sex act and will not be able to hide his failure." Yet for women: "Lack of orgasm does not prevent her ability to participate in the sex act. It cannot be denied that this basic physiological difference may well have a great influence on the degree of confidence which the two sexes have in the possible success of concealment and thus on their character pattern in this respect" (1950, 10).

In addition, Pollak declared that women concealed menstruation. Thus, the biology of women and its impact on sexuality and menstruation made "concealment and misrepresentation in the eyes of women socially required and commendable acts . . . [conditioning] them to a different attitude toward veracity than men" (1950, 10). Pollak's *The Criminality of Women* became so popular that it was reprinted numerous times and cited uncritically for the next twenty years (Rafter and Gibson 2004).

Thus, the missing woman in criminology was granted entry into criminological discourse only as the inferior corporeal woman. Until the early 1970s, sociological criminologists constructed an "essential difference" that equated women with "the natural body" and men with "the social mind." Reflecting the presuppositions already in place in U.S. gender relations, sociological criminologists conceptualized the cause of male crime as *outside* the body and the cause of female crime as *inside* the body. Thus, the rise of sociological criminology rested on the culture–nature, mind–body, and social man–corporeal woman binaries. And although Lombroso's alleged atavistic stigmata found on the surface of the body had now all but disappeared, in sociological criminology the female body remained "Other": biologically enigmatic, afflicted, deceitful, and therefore, in need of pervasive social control by men. Indeed, Sutherland, Pollak, and other sociological criminologists were not dissimilar from sociologists in general, who, prior to the 1970s, developed a "masculine ontology of social being." Sociology as an academic discipline—and resultantly sociological criminology—emerged through a process whereby "women are locked into and overwhelmed by their corporeality, whilst men rise above it and are defined, determined and distinguished by their sociality" (Witz and Marshall 2003, 351).

• 2 •

GENDERED WOMAN, GENDERED MAN

S econd-wave feminism was stimulated by Simone de Beauvoir's well-known argument in *The Second Sex*: "One is not born but rather becomes a woman." As
de Beauvoir pointed out: "biological fate" does not "determine the figure that the
human being presents in society; it is civilization as a whole that produces this
creature indeterminate between male and eunuch which is described as feminine"
(1972, 295). De Beauvoir argued that the social—not the biological—determines
women's situation; that is, women are embedded socially in unequal patriarchal
gender relations where they are compelled "to assume the status of Other" (1972,
29). Indeed, it is not "hormones" or "mysterious instincts" that determine
women's destiny, "but the manner in which her body and her relation to the world
are modified through the action of others than herself" (1972, 734).

THE SEX-GENDER BINARY

Despite de Beauvoir's tremendous influence, it was Ann Oakley who eventually
made a more thoroughgoing distinction between "sex" and "gender" in her
book, *Sex, Gender, and Society* (1972). Oakley defined "sex" as the *biological*
differences between men and women (genitalia and reproductive capacities that
are allegedly universal and immutable) and "gender" as the *social* differences associated with each sex ("masculinity" and "femininity" that are variable and culturally mutable). Thus, in confronting the culture–nature and social man–
corporeal woman binaries, second-wave feminists created a new binary, an off-
shoot of the mind–body dualism—the sex–gender distinction.

Equipped with de Beauvoir's analysis of women's oppression in patriarchal society and Oakley's sex–gender binary, feminist sociological criminologists redefined women's condition—and thus involvement in crime—in social rather than in biological terms. As Nicole Hahn Rafter and Frances Heidensohn (1995, 3) pointed out in their discussion of the development of feminist perspectives on crime, the distinction between "sex" and "gender" made clear that "gender subordination was neither inborn nor inevitable. Once made, the sex–gender distinction enabled feminists to break free of crippling roles and eventually to imagine cultures in which sexual and gender identities might be mixed, matched, and even multiplied."

Early feminist criminologists of the second wave then shifted the analysis of women and crime—as Sutherland had done for men and crime—from biological determinism to social determinism; from the *body* to the *mind*. For feminists there is nothing distinctive about women's biology that causes women's subordination; rather, inequality between men and women is a socially learned and gendered phenomenon that can be socially unlearned and, therefore, changed. Indeed, throughout the 1970s and into the 1980s, feminist sociological criminologists concentrated on criticizing criminological theory for being gender-blind, for misrepresenting women, and for being unable to account sociologically for women and crime. As Eileen Leonard (1982, 1–2) concluded after an exhaustive analysis of criminological theory:

> Theoretical criminology was constructed by men, about men. It is simply not up to the analytical task of explaining female patterns of crime. Although some theories work better than others, they all illustrate what social scientists are slowly recognizing within criminology and outside the field: that our theories are not the general explanations of human behavior they claim to be, but rather particular understandings of male behavior.

Paradoxically, Leonard's argument for a special theory of women's and girls' crime rests on the assumption about difference—that women's lives are fundamentally different from men's—and that it is precisely this social difference that requires illumination. According to early feminist sociological criminologists, then, to properly conceptualize women's relationships to crime there must be a concentration on gender difference embedded in unequal gender relations; that is, how gender power relations uniquely impact women's and girls' social experiences. By the late 1980s, Kathleen Daly and Meda Chesney-Lind (1988, 108) outlined the core elements of feminist thought that guided much feminist criminological research and theory building:

1. Gender is not a natural fact but a complex social, historical, and cultural product; it is related to, but not simply derived from, biological sex difference and reproductive capacities.
2. Gender and gender relations order social life and social institutions in fundamental ways.
3. Gender relations and constructs of masculinity and femininity are not symmetrical but are based on an organizing principle of men's superiority and social- and political-economic dominance over women.
4. Systems of knowledge reflect men's views of the natural and social world; the production of knowledge is gendered.
5. Women should be at the center of intellectual inquiry, not peripheral, invisible, or appendages to men.

Assuming a "natural" *sex* dichotomy in society, feminist criminologists have employed these elements of feminist thought to conduct investigations of women's *gendered* lives and experiences in terms of race, class, and sexuality. Second-wave feminist criminologists challenged the masculinist nature of criminology by illuminating the patterns of gendered power that to that point sociological criminology had all but ignored. In particular, feminist criminologists secured a permanent role for feminism in criminology and moved analysis of gendered power and *social woman* (alongside *social man*) to the forefront of much criminological thought. To be sure, since the mid-1970s feminist scholars have spotlighted and thoroughly researched (1) the nature and pervasiveness of violence against women, (2) girls' and women's crimes and the social control of girls and women, and (3) women working in the criminal justice system (Belknap 2000; Chesney-Lind and Pasko 2004; Daly and Maher 1998; Martin and Jurik 1996; Naffine 1995). The importance of this feminist work is enormous. It has contributed significantly to the discipline of criminology and has made a lasting impact—the importance of gender in understanding the differences in crime by men and women is acknowledged more broadly now within the discipline.

Moreover, the second-wave feminist criminological turn to gender not only illuminated sociological issues unknown previously about women, crime, and social control, it has led also, logically, to the critical study of masculinity and crime. Boys and men are seen no longer as the "normal subjects"; rather, the social construction of masculinities has come under careful criminological scrutiny. In recent years there has emerged a new and growing sociological interest in the relationship among men, masculinities, and crime. Since the early 1990s, numerous works have been published, from individually authored books

(Collier 1998; Hobbs 1995; Messerschmidt 1993, 1997, 2000; Polk 1994; Winlow 2001), to edited volumes (Bowker 1998; Newburn and Stanko 1994; Sabo, Kupers, and London 2001), to special academic journal issues (Carlen and Jefferson 1996; Connell 2002a). This development makes perfect sense because if gender is conceptualized in terms of power relations, it becomes necessary to study not simply the powerless but also the powerful. As with any structure of power and inequality (such as race and class), it is essential to study the powerful. Indeed, the gendered practices of men and boys raise significant questions about crime. Men and boys dominate crime. Arrest, self-report, and victimization data reflect that men and boys perpetrate more conventional crimes—and the more serious of these crimes—than do women and girls. Moreover, men have a virtual monopoly on the commission of syndicated, corporate, and political crime. To be sure, criminologists have consistently advanced gender as the strongest predictor of criminal involvement. Consequently, studying masculinities provides insights into understanding both the highly gendered ratio of crime and crime by individuals in society. Thus, among criminologists interested in gender and crime, what have emerged are studies examining differences in crime between women and men based on *gendered woman* (femininities) and *gendered man* (masculinities).

Nevertheless, conceptualizing a relationship between social and gendered processes and crime—although an important and essential theoretical development within sociological criminology—has caused a disadvantageous aftereffect that has prompted sociological criminologists (feminist and nonfeminist alike) to ignore how those who engage in crime (both men and women) interact with and through their bodies. Both feminist and nonfeminist sociological criminologists established (at different times) and continue to maintain (in different ways) specific types of perspectives on crime in which the body is completely untheorized, as the concentration is on the gendered mind. Consequently, there has developed an inevitable reluctance by sociological criminologists to incorporate in their theories aspects of human embodiment.[1]

Sociological criminology generally rejected the body as a domain for theoretical and empirical enquiry, yet from the very beginning of second-wave feminism the body became a political issue as women struggled to gain control over their bodies. Recent academic feminist empirical and theoretical work outside criminology has addressed, for example, how women experience their bodies, how women's bodies are implicated in various social and cultural practices, symbolic representations of women's bodies, and how cultural discourses shape women's embodied experiences (Daly 1997; Davis 1997, 5; Morgan and Scott 1993). And as Kathy Davis (1997, 10) points out, feminist scholarship has linked women's embodied experience with practices of gendered power: "From the sexualization of the female body in advertising to the mass rape of women in wartime, women's bodies have been subjected to processes of exploitation, inferiorization, exclusion, control and violence."

Although feminist criminologists have also extensively shown the ways in which girls' and women's bodies are exploited, harmed, and dominated under unequal gender relations, they have never confronted—to use Daly and Chesney-Lind's words cited above—how gender is "related to biological sex difference and reproductive capacities." As Judith Allen noted in 1989, feminist criminologists have criticized criminology's historically inadequate analysis of the causes of women's and men's crimes, yet they have endorsed simultaneously the mind–body and sex–gender binaries. This endorsement positively enabled a move to conceptualizing gendered woman and gendered man, yet use of these binaries removed any link between the body and gender; indeed, any notion of the "gendered body" has been rendered arbitrary. Although the sex–gender distinction allowed feminist criminologists to investigate women's and men's social and gendered experiences without reverting to biological determinism, for these feminists gender was constructed socially but the body was not; therefore, the body remained an "under-theorized backdrop" within feminist criminology (Davis 1997, 8).

Consequently, feminist criminologists have, as have sociological criminologists generally since Sutherland, "constructed the body as fixed, immutable, static and utterly outside culture" (Allen 1989, 34). Feminist and profeminist criminologists historically have neglected how social action, lived experience, and crime are embodied. Not only have feminist and profeminist criminologists concentrated on gender *differences* in crime—thereby ignoring possible gender *similarities* in crime—they have also conceptualized the body as a "natural" phenomenon that lies outside their analytical concerns.[2] And the most "popular" theoretical perspectives on gender and crime—John Hagan's (1989) "power-control theory" and Robert Agnew's (1992; 2001) "general strain theory"—likewise completely eschew the body and concentrate solely on gender differences in crime, thereby reproducing the mind–body and sex–gender binaries. Let's briefly review these two perspectives.

DUALIST CRIMINOLOGIES

Hagan (1989) argues that in industrialized societies an instrument–object relationship exists between parents and children. Parents are the instruments of control and its objects are children, and this relationship shapes the social reproduction of gender. However, these power relationships vary by class and by gender. In particular, as women increasingly enter the labor market, they gain "new power in the family" (Hagan 1989, 156).

Hagan identifies two family structures based on women's participation in the paid labor market: "patriarchal" and "egalitarian." In patriarchal families, the husband/father works outside the home in an authority position and the wife/mother works at home. Patriarchal families, through gender-role socialization, "reproduce daughters who focus their futures around domestic labor and consumption, as contrasted with sons who are prepared for participation in direct production" (Hagan 1989, 156). In egalitarian families, the husband/father and wife/mother both work in authority positions outside the home. These egalitarian families "socially reproduce daughters who are prepared along with sons to join the production sphere" (Hagan 1989, 157).

Thus, although in both types of families daughters are less criminal than sons because daughters are more controlled by their mothers, Hagan argues that daughters in patriarchal families are more often taught by parents to avoid risk-taking endeavors, whereas in egalitarian families, both daughters and sons frequently are taught to be more open to risk-taking. It is this combination of the instrument–object relationship and corresponding socialization of risk-taking that affects delinquency. According to Hagan, patriarchal families are characterized by large gender differences in delinquent behavior, whereas egalitarian families maintain smaller gender differences in delinquency: "Daughters become more like sons in their involvement in such forms of risk-taking as delinquency" (1989, 158). Thus, sons (and bodies) are for the most part ignored in this theory, and gender differences in crime are explained by a concentration on the characteristics of mothers and daughters.

In the most recent statement of power-control theory, the emphasis remains exclusively on gender differences in crime, arguing that four conditions result in male overinvolvement in crime (Hagan, McCarthy, and Foster 2002, 43):

(1) a greater degree of freedom from the controls of parental agency; (2) more exposure to and support for master schemas that define activities as gender specific and legitimize male independence; (3) a greater preference for a risk-seeking approach to life; and (4) a stronger conviction that one is unlikely to experience negative consequences for engaging in risky activities.

Thus, for Hagan and his colleagues, the body and gender similarities in crime are theoretically irrelevant.

Agnew (1992) identifies three forms of "strain" that may lead to delinquency: the failure to achieve positively valued goals (such as disjunctions between expectations and actual achievements), the removal of positively valued stimuli from the individual (such as loss of a girlfriend or boyfriend or death of a parent), and the presence of negative stimuli (such as child abuse and neglect or negative relations with parents). In examining strain specifically in relation to gender and crime, Agnew (2001) concentrates on the question: Why do men have a higher crime rate than women? Answer: This is *not* due to men having higher levels of strain than women; in fact, women experience as much if not more strain than men. Instead, men experience different *types* of strain than women, and these are more likely to lead to crime. For example, Agnew (2001, 168) argues that because of gender-role socialization "[m]ales are more concerned with material success and extrinsic achievements, while females are more concerned with the establishment and maintenance of close relationships and with meaning and purpose in life." Such differences in strain, Agnew (2001, 169) argues, explain the greater rate of property crime among men. Moreover, there are important additional differences in social control and gender-role socialization:

> Females are more likely to experience strains like the excessive demands of family members and restrictions on their behavior, with females being more likely to be confined to the "private sphere." These types of strain involve a restriction of criminal opportunities and excessive social control. It is difficult to engage in serious violent and property crime when one spends little time in public, feels responsible for children and others, is burdened with the demands of others, and is under much pressure to avoid behaving in an aggressive manner.

Because men are more likely to be in public and, therefore, to experience conflict with others and criminal victimization, they are more likely to be involved in violence. Thus, the different types of strain men and women experience result in higher rates of crime by the former.

However, Agnew does not stop there, but adds that men and women also differ in their emotional response to strain. Given that strain leads to certain negative emotions—such as anger—this in turn creates pressure to take corrective action. Although both men and women respond to strain with anger, they differ in their experience of anger—women's anger often is accompanied by emotions like fear and depression whereas men's anger more often is characterized by moral outrage. In explaining these differences, Agnew (2001, 169), like Hagan, concentrates on gender-role theory, arguing that by reason of differences in "the socialization process," women learn to blame themselves for negative treatment by others and view their anger as inappropriate and a failure of self-control; men blame others for their negative treatment and view their anger "as an affirmation of their masculinity." Consequently, men are more likely to commit violent and property crimes, whereas women are more likely to resort to self-destructive forms of deviance, such as drug use and eating disorders.

For Hagan and Agnew, then, gendered behavior ultimately is learned through interaction in an unequal culture, and such social conditions affecting the mind give rise to differences in control and strain experienced. Clearly both theoretical conceptualizations present interesting insights on gender and crime, and these insights present an opportunity for a politics of reform as well.

Nevertheless, these theorists' strict distinction between "sex" and "gender" (and thereby "body" and "mind") results in the former being excluded from analysis—they are unable to conceptualize any possible relationship between the body and social practice. In viewing "sex" and the body as unchanging "natural" realities that need no further explanation, power-control and strain theories construct a dualist criminology by neglecting how crime is *embodied* and how the body itself is a material and necessary component of social action. These theories simply are *disembodied*—the body is located outside their conceptual arena—and therefore they have no perception of the body's relation to gender and to crime. Indeed, the body is assumed to be passive and neutral when in fact it is an inescapable and material component of gender. As Alison Assiter (1996, 117) puts it: "One cannot isolate thought and give it expression independently of its embodiment in a living subject."

Additionally, power-control and strain theories distort actual variability in gender constructions and reduce all masculinities and femininities to one normative standard case for each—the "male gender role" and the "female gender role." Concentrating on the differences between men and women, power-control and strain theories ignore the similarities between men and women and disregard the differences among men and boys as well as among women and girls in the construction of gender and crime. Not only are there differences cross-culturally, but within each particular society masculine and feminine practices by men and by women are constructed on the basis of class, race, age, sexuality, and particular social situation, such as the school, peer or leisure group, family, and workplace. The variations in the construction of masculinity and femininity are crucial to understanding the different types and amounts of crime. Power-control and strain theories require that we examine masculinity exclusively by men and boys and femininity by women and girls, thus ignoring *masculinities and femininities by people:* the way individuals (both boys and men and girls and women) construct masculinity and femininity differently.

Thus, both feminist criminological scholars and gender theorists (such as Hagan and Agnew) generally have missed what must be acknowledged—women and girls also construct masculine practices that are related to crime. For example, when we examine different contexts—even within the same milieu—we can conceptualize situations where gender difference is highly salient when compared to those situations in which gender difference is relatively insignificant (Thorne 1993). Power-control and strain theories overlook the salience and fluidity of gender and the diverse ways individuals construct gender in different situations. That is, these theories are capable only of "seeing" gender differences in crime (which is important), but thereby are incapable of explaining gender similarities in crime. Consequently, sometimes commonalities across genders occur whereby women and girls, through engagement in crime, construct masculine conduct. Gender perspectives that concentrate solely on difference are hard put to explain the following by a member of the Turban Queens, a "girl" gang in New York City:

> But once you're in a fight, you just think—you've got to fuck that girl up before she does it to you. You've got to really blow off on her. You just play it crazy. That's when they get scared of you. It's true—you feel proud when you see a girl you fucked up. Her face is all scratched or she got a black eye, you say, "Damn, I beat the shit out of that girl, you know." (Campbell 1991, 262)

Such violence becomes incomprehensible in an analysis that concentrates exclusively on gender differences. Departures from what is considered "appropriate female crime" are ignored—indeed, there is a dearth of theorizing about girls, women, gender, and violence in sociological criminology.[3]

A major result then of an exclusive concentration on gender difference among sociological criminologists has been to direct research and theory in sociological criminology away from issues that seriously complicate difference, such as when girls and women engage in what has traditionally been defined as "male crime." Accordingly, such approaches obscure a full and complete situational understanding of gender and crime: where gender differences in crime are the exclusive focus, similarities in crime often are ignored or misrepresented. Abstracting gender from its social context and insensitive to issues of agency, such perspectives mask the possibility that gender patterns of crime may vary situationally, and that occasionally girls and women and boys and men engage in similar types and amounts of crime. As Karlene Faith (1993, 57) declared in a discussion of women and crime, to concentrate solely on crimes consistent with emphasized femininity "is to deny women's diversity and to promote gender-based objectification and stereotyping." And, as Jody Miller (2002, 441) recently noted: "Selective attention to difference results in the argument that women's actions are always an articulation of 'femininity' and men's of 'masculinity,' even when oppositional or diverse femininities and masculinities are being described and even when there is behavioral similarity across gender."

Given that masculinities and femininities are not determined biologically—although the *lived body* is an inescapable aspect of gender—it certainly makes sense to identify and examine possible masculinities by women and girls (and femininities by men and boys) and their relation to crime. Indeed, there remains a necessity in criminological research to uncover not only gender diversity among girls and women, but also girls' and women's relations to crime and violence and whether or not such social action constructs masculinity or femininity.

Finally, power-control and strain theories additionally describe men and women simply as "passive vessels" into which a variety of gendered expectations are poured. In their reliance on gender-role theory, individuals resultantly display little if any creativity; their actions, including crime, are the result of their socialized gender role—gender simply is internalized in the mind, and becomes resolute and unvarying. This reliance ignores the fact that men and women are active agents in their social relations, and fails to account for the intentions of social actors, how social action is often—but not always—a meaningful construction in itself, and how individuals may reinterpret, resist, or subvert "gender roles." In other words, the above theories "obscure the work that is involved in producing gender in everyday activities" (West and Zimmerman 1987, 127). Gender is not simply shaped and established beforehand, it is accomplished through embodied social action, and sometimes in ways that challenge culturally "appropriate" patterns (Thorne 1993). Indeed, individuals (men *and* women) actively negotiate specific types of masculinity and femininity out of social settings—and subsequent resources at their disposal—in which they find themselves.

For all these reasons, then, power-control and strain theories are unsuitable to our task: they construct more enigmas than they resolve, especially concerning the body and its relation to gender and violence. Indeed, in disembodying gender and crime these theories create the impression that the body is a "natural" unchanging object that exists apart from the social, and is discoverable only through the efforts of natural scientists, not social scientists. Moreover, in their concentration on a binary conception of gender and crime, these theories are haunted by the reality of diversity and by the occasional similarities between men and women in crime. In short, power-control and strain perspectives—as well as sociological criminologists in general—construct a dualist criminology engendering the mind–body, sex–gender and gender difference binaries.

DECONSTRUCTING "NATURAL" BODIES

In an important 1978 article, Neal Shover and Stephen Norland showed that criminologists bring to their work on crime a set of gendered stereotypes, and then proceed to discern empirical patterns and construct theoretical explanations consistent with their beliefs. The discipline has not changed. As demonstrated throughout this chapter, sociological criminologists (feminist and nonfeminist alike) assume ab initio that there exists but two "natural" sexes (male and female) and, therefore, but two genders (masculine and feminine). This assumption is grounded in a specific cultural framework that views sex as strictly dichotomous and unchanging. And sociological criminologists are not alone. In their critique of research on biology and gender, for example, Suzanne Kessler and Wendy McKenna report that as natural scientists engage in the social practice of biological research, they always begin with a conception of "man" and "woman." That is, natural scientists justify and appear to provide grounds for "the already existing knowledge that a person is either a woman or a man and that there is no problem differentiating between the two" (1978, 163).

We therefore should not be surprised that contemporary sociological criminologists begin with the assumption that there are only two sexes, and then proceed to find evidence supporting that assumption. Criminologists have addressed the problem of the gendered nature of crime through a theoretical lens that assumes that "sex" is exclusively dichotomous when no such dichotomy holds biologically, historically, cross-culturally, or even currently within Western societies such as the United States. For example, chromosomes are seen as a critical biological criterion for determining sex. If there is at least one Y chromosome, the individual is male; if there are no Y chromosomes, the individual is female. Yet as Kessler and McKenna demonstrate, there exist people who are genetic mosaics (individuals with XO, XXY, or XXXX chromosomes, for example). So what is their sex? Chromosomal testing in the Olympic games provides the answer: All mosaics are declared men and may participate only in "male" events and the "sex" dichotomy is preserved (1978, 52–54).

Historical research likewise problematizes the notion of a "natural" unchanging sex dichotomy, which we explored in chapter 1 when discussing the important work of Thomas Laqueur (1990). More recently, in *Beyond the Natural Body*, Nelly Oudshoorn (1994) shows that conceptualizations of "sex" by natural scientists are, not surprisingly, read through gender. Oudshoorn examines the historic rise of endocrinology and how hormones were first "seen" by natural scientists as the material *truth* of sex difference. Not only did these scientists define hormones differently among each other—"the hormone of the biochemist is . . . quite different from the hormone of the biologist" (1994, 36)—but Oudshoorn shows how "scientific facts" about sex hormones are constructed socially and then, in the not too distant future, dissolved socially. Natural scientists struggled incisively in the 1920s and 1930s to discover distinct sex hormones, only later to find "male hormones" in women's bodies and "female hormones" in men's bodies. In other words, despite differences among natural scientists, they were all similar, Oudshoorn argued, in beginning their research with a conception of sex differences and in persisting to search for and locate evidence of such difference, only to discern later that their "proof" was a frivolous social construction. Indeed, both testosterone and estrogen are present in all human bodies (many women have higher levels of the former than many men) "and after age fifty, men on average have higher levels of estrogen in their blood- stream than women" (Connell 2002a, 33). Thus, we should not be surprised to find Anthony Giddens (1989, 286) arguing that "[t]here is not a single physical char- acteristic, or even combination of physical characteristics, which cleanly and com- pletely separates 'women' from 'men.'" And as Gisela Kaplan and Lesley Rogers (1990, 214) argue after a careful examination of biological studies on "sex": "The rigid either/or assignment of the sexes is only a convenient social construct, not a bi- ological reality." This does not mean, of course, that the body is not an existing ma- terial phenomenon—it is. However, certain anatomical and physiological criteria are "seen" historically and socially and, therefore, are constructed so as to buttress the sex dichotomy. As Simon Williams and Gillian Bendelow (1998, 116) put it, what is conceptualized as "sex" is always "mediated by our existence as *social* be- ings and *historical* agents."

Regarding cross-culture, anthropological evidence reveals that in other soci- eties "sex" is not always dichotomous and is not always assigned on the basis of biological criteria. Whereas in Western industrialized societies the ultimate cri- terion for sex assignment is genitalia, in several other societies it is strictly social activities. M. Kay Martin and Barbara Voorhies (1975), for example, found that certain societies recognize more than two sex statuses and that in these societies sex is not assigned on the basis of physical criteria (e.g., genitalia). In this regard, consider the following account of the Nuer of East Africa, which indicates that a woman who remains childless a certain number of years is considered sterile (Heritier-Auge 1989, 294):

> [She] returns to her own family, where from then on she is considered a man— "brother" to her brothers, paternal "uncle" to her brothers' children. As an "un- cle" she will be in a position to build up a herd, just like a man, from her share of the cattle paid as a bride price on her nieces. With this herd and the fruits of her personal industry, she will in turn be able to pay the bride price for one or several

wives. She enters into these institutionalized matrimonial relations as the "husband." Her wives wait on her, work for her, honor her, show her the courtesies due a husband. She hires a [male] servant of another ethnic group, usually a Dinka, of whom she demands services including sexual services for her wife or wives. The children born of these relations are hers, call her "father" and treat her the way one treats a male father.

In other words, for the Nuer, a sterile woman becomes a "man" and thus it is *fertility* that determines "sex" in this particular society (Heritier-Auge 1989, 295).

Morcover, in the Sambia of Papua New Guinea, Gilbert Herdt (1994) found a "three-sex model" in which the "third sex" is neither male nor female, but labeled *kwolu-aatmwol*. The Sambia determine sex through genitalia; their third sex is what Western societies label the "intersexed" or "hermaphroditism." Although a masculine dominated culture, the third sex is accepted into Sambian society and may even become, for example, distinguished shamans and warriors. As Herdt (1994, 437) concludes: "The *kwolu-aatmwol* is not therefore rejected or frozen out of daily and normative social contacts and may indeed rise to distinction through special achievements."

In addition to the existence of more than two sexes, numerous societies maintain multiple gender systems in which third and fourth genders exist. For example, the *xanith* of the Omani Muslims (Wikan 1984), the *Hijras* of India (Nanda 1990), and the Tahitian *mahu* (Gilmore 1990) are all examples of a third gender that operates outside the Westernized masculine/feminine dichotomy. Moreover, with regard to Native American societies Will Roscoe (1998, 7) shows that a male third gender (commonly referred to as *berdache*, who became "social women") has been documented in over 155 tribes, and in approximately one-third of these groups, "a formal status also existed for females who undertook a man's lifestyle, becoming hunters, warriors, and chiefs." In such Native American societies the women constituted a fourth gender, identified with special terms—*bote* in Crow, *nadleehi* in Navajo, *winkte* in Lakota, and *hwame* in Mohave (Roscoe 1998, 7).

In contemporary Western societies such as the United States, on the basis of genitalia alone it has been suggested that there exist at least five sexes, three sexual orientations, five gender displays, six types of relationships, and ten self-identifications (Lorber 1994). As Bob Connell (2002a, 36) remarks in response to these variations: "Leaving aside the five sexes, that makes, if my arithmetic is correct, 900 different gender situations one can be in. So much for 'dimorphism.'" Moreover, often when "violations" of the sex dichotomy occur—such as in the case of the "intersexed"—Western societies (distinguished from the Sambia) surgically "correct" the problem, and thus reproduce the dichotomy. Kessler's (1990) study of the role physicians play in cases of intersexed infants shows clearly how these physicians engage in practices designed to ensure infants' physical conformity to the culturally ordained sex dichotomy. Born with ambiguous genitalia, intersexed infants are socially assigned one of two sexes by the attending physician. For example, if the physician feels he or she can reconstruct a "micropenis" into an "adequate-sized penis," the infant will be assigned "male." If it is determined the reconstruction is impossible, the infant will be assigned "female." Thus, medical doctors socially construct "sex." As Kessler (1990, 24) expresses it:

> Although the deformity of intersexed genitals would be immutable were it not for medical interference, physicians do not consider it natural. Instead they think of, and speak of, the surgical/hormonal alteration of such deformities as natural because such intervention returns the body to what it "ought to have been" if events had taken their typical course. The non-normative is converted into the normative, and the normative state is considered natural. The genital ambiguity is remedied to conform to a "natural," that is, culturally indisputable, gender dichotomy.

Similar processes occur when criminologists construct biological explanations of crime. For example, David Rowe argues in his book *Biology and Crime* that the much higher rates of violence by men relative to women is the result of evolutionary "sexual selection" in which men's bodies—"on average men are taller and stronger than women"—are "adapted for greater use of threat and violence against others" (2002, 49). Whereas men allegedly are "adapted" for higher rates of physical violence, women allegedly are "adapted" for verbal violence, such as "backbiting and gossip among women as forms of aggression . . . [which] can inflict damage on the reputation and status of rivals for a woman's romantic partner." Unable to provide empirical evidence of such alleged sexual selection, Rowe resorts to pure speculation:

> To account for these differences in physical characteristics and behavior, *we must suppose* that those males who used aggressive tactics in the Pleistocene had greater reproductive success than nonaggressive males did. . . . *We do not know*, of course, whether this advantage has existed in every generation, extending back thousands of years. However, *it must have existed* frequently enough to produce the visible sexual dimorphism between men and women. (2002, 50; emphasis added)

Rowe begins with an interpretation of current gender patterns of violence and then posits "sexual selection" to justify the pattern. Unable to explain women's involvement in physical violence (for Rowe, women are aggressive exclusively in a verbal way and for only sexual reasons) as well as nonviolence among most men, Rowe's conception of what is "natural" and of what "natural sex differences" consist is a social construct, embedded in contemporary binary assumptions about "maleness" and "femaleness." Moreover, his emphasis on physical sex *difference* ignores the fact that physical differences are considerably more pronounced *within* the sexes and that distributions between the sexes substantially *overlap*. As Connell (1987, 80) points out:

> The members of either sex vary tremendously in height, strength, endurance, dexterity and so on [and] the distributions of the two sexes overlap to a great extent. Social practices that construct women and men as distinct categories by converting an average difference into a categorical difference—"men are stronger than women"—negate the major pattern of difference that occurs within sexes rather than between them.

In short, the resulting gross exaggeration of differences between men and women through gendered social practice occurs precisely because "the biological logic" is unable to "sustain the gender categories" (Connell 1987, 81).[4]

DECONSTRUCTING DISCURSIVE BODIES

In light of the fact that, as Ann Oakley (1997, 30) now concedes—"Ultimately sex is no more natural than gender"—in the mid- to late-1990s postmodern feminist scholars began to consider seriously the theoretical importance of the body by following Foucault's (1979) argument that the body is a malleable phenomena that is produced by, and exists within, discourse. In criminology, the work of Alison Young (1996) and Richard Collier (1998) are notable in this regard.

Young's impressive and powerful book *Imagining Crime* examines the discourses constructed by, for example, criminal justice personnel, criminologists, and journalists. Through analysis of discourses, Young concludes that "textual outlaws"—such as murderous children—are the sacrificial lambs fashioned to maintain a false sense of community: "a phantasm that speaks of a nostalgic desire for oneness and unity, while at the same time structuring itself around its dependence upon fear, alienation and separateness for its elements to make sense" (1996, 10). But in addition, "femininity" is also phantasm in the sense that it is "both known and unknown for criminology. It is unknown in that it can only ever register in criminology's symbolic order as the inverted negation of masculinity. It is known in that it is continually measured, recorded, examined and inspected for evidence of its necessary deviance, its waywardness" (1996, 27).

The body is an important aspect of Young's thesis and, as she argues, is accessible only through language "as spectacle to be consumed, disciplined, repressed" (1996, 17). Young argues that representations and cultural inscriptions—that is, discourse—constitute bodies and produce bodies. As an example of such discourse, consider Young's analysis of the well-known 1993 abduction and torturous murder of two-year-old James Bulger by two ten-year-old boys in England (1996, 111–146). Concerned with the discourse of the national press, Young convincingly showed how journalists constructed James as embodying the ideals of childhood—such as innocence—whereas the two ten-year-old boys were characterized "naturally" as "monsters in disguise." The press discourse then distinguished child from nonchild in how embodiment of victim and offender were represented. Consequently, the "imagination" of crime, Young concluded, is in part a result of the media demonization of the body of the criminal that removes any community responsibility for the heinous acts.

Richard Collier's feminist-inspired work on masculinities and crime—*Masculinities, Crime, and Criminology: Men, Heterosexuality and the Criminal(ised) Other*—similarly argues that the body is constituted in discourse and made to "signify" in particular ways and at particular moments by discourse. The bulk of Collier's book describes the ways in which various "male subjects"—lawyers, criminologists, youth offenders, mass murderers, and fathers—have been constituted in, and made to signify by, particular discourses. As an example, Collier explored the discursive production of the "dangerous" boy in contemporary Britain. And like Young, he focused on how adolescent boy offenders have been produced through discourse. Collier discussed the case of the "rat boy" as an example of "dehumanizing the (dangerous) bodies of youth" (1998, 91). The rat boy discourse emerged in Britain due to growing concern (in 1993) over "what to do" with persistent adolescent boy offenders. Rat boys would engage in "crime sprees" and then "hide in a maze of ventilation shafts, tunnels, and roof spaces . . . while trying to evade capture"—hence the name "rat boy" (1998, 92). Various discourses eventually characterized these working-class boys as "monsters," "animals," "vermin," and "as beyond the social, outside society, as venal." According to Collier, what emerged through this discursive characterization was an offending adolescent boy who was simultaneously "sexed" as masculine: "at the very moment that any consideration of the sexed specificity of youth crime itself—the fact that these are overwhelmingly the activities of boys and young men—is being effaced through the making of this association with the 'nonhuman' (the criminal, the feral, and so forth)." In other words, discourse in Britain constructed the adolescent boy offenders' "sexed body" as "like other boys and yet who also [appear] as other, as less than human, as *different* from other boys" (1998, 91).

Both Young's and Collier's discussions of the discursive body are compelling presentations that have proved extremely helpful in proposing the inclusion of the body in sociological criminology and have provided criminology with insight into how bodies can be inscribed through discourse. Indeed, Young and Collier successfully challenged the notion of a "natural" pre-social body by showing that our conceptualization of the "criminal" often is discursively "sexed" in particular ways. Nevertheless, how the body is experienced in everyday life regrettably is overlooked. For Young and Collier, we have access to the body only through analysis of discourse—there is no attempt to problematize the consciously active, practicing lived body. Missing from Young's and Collier's analyses are the social processes and practices through which the body becomes meaningful to the social agent himself or herself; how the body is lived in everyday life disappears, thus forgoing any conceptualization of how crime is actually embodied. Indeed, in Young's and Collier's analyses: "The body is dissolved as a causal phenomenon into the determining power of discourse, and it becomes extremely difficult to conceive of the body as a material component of social action" (Shilling 2003, 71). Young and Collier simply replace a "natural essentialism" with a "discursive essentialism" in the sense that "society is brought so far into the body that the body disappears as a phenomenon that requires detailed historical investigation in its own right. It is present as an item of discussion, but absent as an object of analysis. As the body is whatever discourse constructs it as being, it is discourse rather than the body that needs examining" (Shilling 2003, 71–72).

Moreover, Collier, following Elizabeth Grosz (1994; 1995), actually argues that the concept of *gender* is no longer applicable to criminology. For Grosz (1995, 212) gender is irrelevant and redundant today because *sex*, through discursive inscriptions, is "always already expression, which in itself does not require a second order expression." Thus, "sexed bodies" are the analytic "terrain" that must be examined to uncover the "production and enactment of sexual difference" (Grosz 1995, 213). Similarly, Collier (1998, 24, 25) argues that "in contrast to the focus on the 'gendering' of crime," criminologists should now be exclusively concerned "with the sexing *and* criminalizing (a sexed-criminalizing?) of the bodies of men" (and women) because such an approach "valorizes *sexual difference*." However, there exists at least two problems with a concentration on sexed bodies and therefore sexual difference. First, in such a conceptualization, Collier can speak only of men and masculinity, ignoring the reality that women and girls sometimes engage in masculine practices and crime. As John Hood-Williams (2001, 39) asks: "Are we to believe that the genders really do constitute coherent, uniform categories whose social and psychic consequence is a perfect, homogenous binary?" In other words, there is nothing built into Collier's perspective that allows for girls, women, masculine practices, and crime. Consequently, his perspective—like sociological criminology historically—reifies gender (and "sex") difference. Second, by valorizing "sex" and devalorizing "gender," Collier hastily forfeits feminist criminology's "distinctive conceptual grip on the complex more-than-fleshy sociality that the concept of gender gives a purchase on" (Witz 2000, 6–7). I agree with Collier (and Young) that sociological criminology—and in particular feminist criminology—must "bring the body back in," but it must do so by *embodying gender*, not by "sexing" the criminal. Collier's devalorizing of gender actually constructs the sex–gender distinction in a new and unique way: Whereas for Hagan and Agnew the body is deemed outside their sphere of criminological enquiry, for Collier it is the discursive "sexed body" that is assessed analytic prominence—as gender is now all but inapplicable to any discussion of crime by men and women.

Arguably, this repudiation of the concept "gender" is highly premature, especially given the rich intellectual history of gender analysis by feminist and profeminist sociologists and criminologists since the early 1970s. Indeed, as Connell asserts, if we disavow a "gender analysis," such concepts as "the patriarchal state, rape culture, compulsory heterosexuality, the gender division of labor, and the glass ceiling would be swept away—since all such concepts explain by means of gender and express patterns of causation in gender relations" (1997a, 703). Thus, and specifically regarding criminology, I agree with Meda Chesney-Lind and Lisa Pasko (2004, vii) who recently affirmed that "[g]ender matters in crime and crime policy" and therefore "[g]ender must be theorized in order to do good criminological research." Nevertheless, conceptualizations of gender and its relation to crime must be supplemented by a recuperation of the body, which has been "left sitting uncomfortably on the sidelines of feminist sociology [and criminology], somehow outside or beyond its field of concerns" (Witz 2000, 7).

In sum, the discipline of criminology historically has maintained, in various ways, the mind–body, sex–gender, and gender difference binaries. A satisfactory theory of gender and crime requires therefore not simply a rejection of these binaries, but a specific concentration on (1) embodiment as a *lived* aspect of gender, (2) both *gender differences* and *gender similarities* in the commission of crime, and (3) how embodied social action is embedded in specific structural gender relations in particular settings. It is to this perspective that we turn our attention in part II.

PART II

THEORY AND METHOD

• 3 •

STRUCTURED
ACTION THEORY

The mystery regarding the relationship among the body, gender, and differences and similarities in crime ultimately is not hidden *inside* the fleshiness
of the body but, rather, it is readily understood from the *outside*,
luminously flaunted in our socially embodied practices, interactions, and institutions. As Jean-Paul Sartre (1956, 729) would have put it: There is a mystery,
but it is "a mystery in broad daylight." Thus, I argue in this chapter that the mystery of the relationship between embodied gendered practices and crime can be
revealed by conceptualizing it as a form of "structured action." In examining life-
history data on assaultive violence and nonviolence by both boys and girls[1]—as
I do in parts III and IV—"structured action theory" will provide the means to
investigate (1) embodiment as a *lived* aspect of gender, (2) the possibility of adolescent masculine practices by *both* boys and girls, (3) how such embodied
actions may be related to violence and nonviolence, and (4) the validity of the
mind–body, sex–gender, and gender difference binaries. Accordingly, part II
begins here with a close examination of the distinctive components of structured
action theory, and then, in chapter 4, I outline the methodology used to gather
the data for the adolescent-life stories presented in part III.

DOING GENDER

Reflecting various theoretical origins (Connell 1987, 1995; Giddens 1976,
1984; Goffman 1963, 1972, 1979; Kessler and McKenna 1978; Sartre 1956;
West and Fenstermaker 1995; West and Zimmerman 1987), structured action

theory emphasizes the construction of gender as a situated social, interactional, and embodied accomplishment. In other words, gender grows out of embodied social practices in specific social structural settings and serves to inform such practices in reciprocal relation. Historical and social conditions shape the character and definition of "sex" categories (social identification of birth classification). Sex categories and their meanings are given concrete expression by the specific social relations and historical context in which they are embedded.

In an important work that I mentioned in chapter 2, Suzanne Kessler and Wendy McKenna (1978) argue that gendered social action is constructed through taken-for-granted assumptions, or what they call "incorrigible propositions." Our belief in two objectively real, biologically created constant sexes is a telling incorrigible proposition. We assume there are only two sexes; each person is simply an example of one or the other. In other words, we construct a sex dichotomy in which no dichotomy holds biologically, historically, cross-culturally, and contemporaneously.

The key process in the social construction of the sex dichotomy is what Kessler and McKenna call "gender attribution," or the active (although usually not conscious) way we decide what sex a person is (1978, 1–20). A significant incorrigible proposition of gender attribution is that men have penises, women do not. Thus we consider genitals the ultimate criterion in making sex assignments; yet, in our daily interactions we continually make gender attributions with a complete lack of information about others' genitals. Our recognition of another's sex is dependent upon the exhibit of such bodily characteristics as speech, hair, clothing, physical appearance, and other aspects of personal front—an embodied gender presentation that becomes a substitute for the concealed genitalia.

Nevertheless, as Candace West and Sarah Fenstermaker (1995) argue, "doing gender" entails considerably more than the "social emblems" of sex category. Rather, the social construction of gender involves a situated social, interactional, and embodied accomplishment. Gender grows out of social practices in specific settings and serves to inform such practices in reciprocal relation.[2] Although sex category defines social identification as "male" or "female," "doing gender" systematically corroborates that identification through embodied social interaction. In effect, there is a plurality of forms in which gender is constructed: we coordinate our activities to "do" gender in situational ways (West and Zimmerman 1987).

Accordingly, early gender development in childhood occurs through an interactive process between child and parents, other children, and other adults. By reason of this interaction with others, children undertake to practice what is being preached and represented. Bob Connell defines the proactive adoption of specific embodied gender practices as the "moment of engagement," the moment when an individual takes up a *project* of masculinity or femininity as his or her own (1995, 122). Gender projects are "patterns of a life-course projected from the present into the future, bringing new conditions or events into existence which were not there before" (Connell 2002a, 81). Individuals negotiate the embodied masculine and feminine practices that are prevalent and attributed as such in their particular milieu(s) and, in so doing, commit themselves to a *fundamental* project of masculine or feminine self-attribution—"I'm a boy" or "I'm a girl." This *fundamental gender project* is the primary gendered mode by which individuals choose to relate to the world and to express oneself in it. Indeed, what makes us human is the fact that we construct ourselves by making choices that transcend given circumstances and propel us into a future that is defined by the consequences of those choices (Sartre 1956). As Connell (1987, 211) observes: "Humans project themselves into their future by their choices, by the way they negate and transcend the circumstances that are given to them to start with. The person is constructed as a 'project' of realizing oneself in a particular way."

Doing gender (West and Zimmerman 1987) is a continuing process in which individuals construct patterns of embodied presentations and practices that suggest masculinity or femininity in particular settings and, consequently, project themselves into a future where new situations are encountered and subsequently new choices are made. Indeed, an incorrigible proposition of industrialized societies is the belief in the permanence of gender self-attribution—"Once a boy (or girl) always a boy (or girl)" (Kessler and McKenna 1978, 10). Thus, there exists unity and coherence to one's gender project in the sense that we recognize ourselves as a boy or as a girl and *embody* this particular gendered self over time and space.

Nevertheless, and although individuals construct a fundamental project as either male or female, the actual accomplishment of masculinity and femininity varies situationally—that is, gender is renegotiated continuously through social interaction and, therefore, one's masculine or feminine self may be fraught with contradictions and diversity in gender strategies and practices. Indeed, individuals may situationally adopt cross-gender strategies and engage in certain masculine and feminine practices without changing their fundamental gender project; others may construct a specific fundamental gender project (e.g., masculine) that contradicts their bodily sex category (e.g., female).

Crucial to conceptualizing gender as a situated accomplishment and gender project is the notion of "accountability" (West and Zimmerman 1987). Accountability refers to individuals who configure and orchestrate their embodied actions in relation to how such actions may be interpreted by others in the particular social context in which they occur. In other words, in their daily activities individuals attempt to be identified bodily as "female" or "male." In this way, accountability "allows individuals to conduct their activities in relation to their circumstances," suggesting persuasively that gender varies by social situation (West and Fenstermaker 1995, 156). Within social interaction, then, we encourage and expect others to attribute to us a particular sex category. And we facilitate the ongoing task of accountability through demonstrating that we are male or female by means of concocted practices that may be interpreted accordingly. Consequently, we do gender differently, depending on the social situation and the social circumstances we encounter. The specific meanings of gender are defined in social interaction and therefore through personal practice. Doing gender renders social action accountable in terms of available gender practices appropriate to one's sex category in the specific social situation in which one acts (West and Fenstermaker 1995; Yancey Martin 2003). Thus, it is the particular gender relations in specific settings that give behavior its gendered meaning.

In this view, then, although we decide quite early in life that we're a boy or a girl and, for the most part, maintain that gendered self over the course of our life, the actual everyday "doing" of gender is accomplished systematically and is never a static or a finished product. Rather, people construct gender in specific social situations. In other words, people participate in self-regulating conduct whereby they monitor their own and others' embodied social actions. Doing gender, therefore, does not mean always living up to situationally normative conceptions of femininity and masculinity; rather, "It is to engage in behavior *at the risk of* being held accountable for it" (Fenstermaker and West 2002, 30). This perspective allows for innovation and flexibility in gender construction—and the ongoing potentiality of normative transgression—but also underscores the ever-present *possibility* of any activity being assessed by copresent interactants as either feminine or masculine. Thus, although we construct ourselves as male or female, we situationally embody masculinity and femininity according to our own unique experiences.

Moreover, such social action has further temporal dimensions that impact doing gender. As Jody Miller (2002, 450) has pointed out in an influential contribution to structured action theory, it is essential to examine gendered social action in a variety of ways, including "a focus on rational action that is goal-seeking, purposeful and deliberate; on norm-oriented action or that which is taken in response to normative expectations; on actions that may be viewed as 'resistance,' negotiation or rebellion against norms or inequalities; as well as routinized actions that are largely unreflective or taken for granted." Conceptualizing social action in these various ways allows us to understand the way social practice develops differently based on particular gender relations and social structural conditions.

Related to the above is Patricia Yancey Martin's recent differentiation between "gender practices" and "practicing gender." The term "gender practices" refers to forms of behavior that are "available" in specific social settings for individuals "to enact in an encounter or situation in accord with (or in violation of) the gender institution." In other words, these are potential, situationally available embodied social actions "that people know about and have the capacity or agency to do, assert, perform, or mobilize" (Yancey Martin 2003, 354). The term "practicing gender" entails actually "doing" the situationally available gender practices and is usually accomplished with copresent interactants and often—but not always—nonreflexively. To do gender reflexively individuals must "carefully consider the content of one's actions and act only after careful consideration of the intent, content, and effects of one's behavior" (Yancey Martin 2003, 356). Thus, individuals do gender both while consciously intending to and without consciously intending to, depending upon the particular setting in which they act. Although we make choices to act in particular ways, those choices are based on the situationally available gender practices. And "doing" or "practicing" gender may or may not be consciously intended as a masculine or feminine act. Accountability then encourages people to do gender appropriate to particular situations, but the ultimate choice to do so—or not to do so—may be simply an unreflective routinized action (Yancey Martin 2003).

RELATIONS, STRUCTURES, AND ACTION

As the forgoing indicates, although gender is "made," so to speak, through the variable unification of choice, self-regulated practices, and nonreflexivity, these embodied practices do not occur in a vacuum. Instead, they are influenced by the social structural constraints we experience. Social structures, defined here as regular and patterned forms of interaction over time that constrain and channel behavior in specific ways, "only exist as the reproduced conduct of situated actors" (Giddens 1976, 127). As Connell (1987, 1995) argues, gendered social structures are neither external to social actors nor simply and solely constraining. On the contrary, structure is realized only through embodied social action, and social action requires structure as its condition. "Knowledgeable" human agents of gender practices (Yancey Martin 2003) enact social structures by putting into practice their structured knowledge; yet, in certain circumstances they may improvise or innovate in structurally shaped ways that significantly reconfigure the very structures that shaped them (Giddens 1984). Because people do gender in specific social situations, they reproduce and sometimes change social structures. And given that people often reproduce gender ideals in socially structured specific practices, there are a variety of ways to do them. Within specific social settings particular forms of gender practices are available, encouraged, and permitted, and because the forms depend on one's position in these social relations, we must speak of masculini*ties* and feminini*ties*. Accordingly, gender must be viewed as *embodied structured action*—what people, and therefore bodies, do under specific social structural constraints (Messerschmidt 1993, 1997, 2000). The key to understanding the maintenance of existing gendered social structures is the accomplishment of gender through embodied social interaction—the doing or practicing of gender (Fenstermaker and West 2002; Yancey Martin 2003). Social actors perpetuate and transform social structures within the same interaction; simultaneously, these structures constrain and enable gendered social action. The result is the ongoing social construction of gender relations.

Structured action theory, then, is specifically relevant to the study of teenage violence and nonviolence. As James Short (1982, 4) concludes after reviewing criminological literature on violent crime: "The linkage of . . . micro- and macrosocial levels of explanation is vital to the understanding and explanation of violent crime." That is, theory that connects social action (micro) with social structure (macro) is essential to the comprehension of adolescent violence. Indeed, as Connell (2002a, 82) points out, through negotiations with the constraints and enabling aspects of social structures, the individual "improvises, copies, creates, and thus develops characteristic strategies for handling situations in which gender relations are present. . . . Over time, especially if the strategies are successful, they become settled, crystallizing as specific patterns of femininity or masculinity."

Social structures influence practice so that some gender strategies are more successful than others. Accordingly, and as noted earlier, there is likely to be a degree of social standardization of individual gendered lives—we consistently over time and space construct ourselves as "a boy" or as "a girl." Nevertheless, people may develop several gender strategies at the same time. Thus, a gender project involves "a number of distinct *moments* or *stages* in which different gender commitments are made, different strategies are adopted, or different resolution of gender issues are achieved" (Connell 2002a, 83)—depending upon the particular social structures and, therefore, gender practices prevalent in one's social milieu.

THE SALIENCE OF GENDER, RACE, CLASS, AND SEXUALITY

The salience of gender relations to influencing crime varies by social situation. Although gender construction is ubiquitous, the significance of gender shifts from context to context: in one situation gender may be important to actuating crime; in another, class, race, or other social variables (such as sexual preference) may be more important. In other words, gender is not absolute and is not always significant in every social setting in which crime is realized. As Barrie Thorne (1993, 85) notes:

> A boy may always be a "boy," and that fact will enter into all of his experiences. But in some interactions he may be much more aware of that strand of his identity than in others, just as his ethnicity or age may be more relevant in some situations than in others. Multiple identities may also compound one another; sometimes it is highly salient that one is an African-American boy.

Indeed, structured action theory is not a general theory of crime because masculinity and femininity vary in salience by social situation (Alder and Polk 1996; Messerschmidt 1997). Nevertheless, social relations of gender—like class, race, and sexuality—variously join us in a common relationship to others: we share gendered structural space. Consequently, common or shared blocks of gendered knowledge about gender practices evolve through interaction in which particular gender ideals and activities differ in significance. Through such interaction, gender becomes institutionalized, permitting, for example, men and women to draw on such existing but previously formed ways of doing or practicing gender to construct particular gender strategies for specific settings. The particular criteria of masculinity and femininity thus are embedded in the social situations and recurrent practices by which gender relations are structured (Giddens 1989; Yancey Martin 2003). Nevertheless, accountability to gender is not always, in every social situation, critical to the social construction of crime. Thus, I emphasize in this book certain social situations in which gendered practices are highly salient to the commission of assaultive violence and nonviolence by white working-class adolescent boys and girls.

POWER, DIFFERENCE, AND SIMILARITY

Power is an important structural feature of gender relations. Socially organized power relations among men and women are constructed historically on the bases of race, class, and sexual preference. In other words, in specific contexts some men and some women have greater power than other men or other women; the capacity to exercise power and do gender is, for the most part, a reflection of one's *place* in gender relations. For example, in the antebellum South, "[w]hite men as husbands had control over their wives and as fathers control over their children's marriages and access to family property, but black slaves had no such patriarchal rights" (Ferguson 1991, 113). Moreover, in late nineteenth- and twentieth-century California and Hawaii, most domestic servants in white, middle-class households were Asian men who were subordinate to both white men and white women (Glenn 1992). Consequently, *in general* heterosexual men and women exercise greater power than do gay men and lesbians; upper-class men and women exercise greater power than do working-class men and women; and white men and women exercise greater power than do racial minority men and women. Power, then, is a relationship that structures social interaction not only between men and women but among men and women as well.

Nevertheless, power is not absolute and at times may actually shift in relation to different axes of power and powerlessness. That is, in one situation a working-class man may, for example, exercise power (e.g., as a patriarchal husband), whereas in another situation he may experience powerlessness (e.g., as a factory worker). Accordingly, masculinity and femininity can be understood only as fluid, relational, and situational constructs; yet the capacity to do gender is a reflection of one's *place* in gender relations.

Connell's (1987, 1995, 2002a) notion of *hegemonic masculinity*—the culturally idealized form of masculinity in a given historical and social setting—is relevant here. For Connell (1987, 183), the power relations between men and women and among men are based on "the global dominance of men over women." Such gendered power is constructed and maintained through hegemonic masculinity, which Connell defines as the "configuration of gender practice which embodies the currently accepted answer to the problem of the legitimacy of patriarchy, which guarantees (or is taken to guarantee) the dominant position of men and the subordination of women" (1995, 77). *Emphasized femininity*—although likewise the culturally idealized form of femininity in a given historical and social setting—is subordinate to hegemonic masculinity because it is "oriented to accommodating the interests and desires of men" (Connell 1987, 183). Other forms of femininity are constructed through a variety of combined strategies of compliance and resistance. Because the construction of femininities cannot avoid the global dominance of men over women, the process of doing femininity "is likely to polarize around compliance or resistance to this dominance" (Connell 1987, 187). Thus, masculinities and femininities entail both the doing of gender and the structural relations of gender. Masculinities and femininities are accomplished according to the structural place one occupies. Focusing on the processes and relationships in which men and women conduct their lives, masculinity and femininity are simultaneously a *place* in gender relations and the *practices* through which people engage that place (Connell 1995).

Hegemonic masculinities vary over time, across societies, and among institutions in society—"[h]egemony has many different configurations, and may be local as distinct from general" (Connell 2002b, 89). Thus, although there exists a variety of hegemonic masculinities, what makes them similar is that in any specific time and place—such as whole societies or particular settings (e.g., schools, families, and peer and leisure groups)—hegemonic masculinities are culturally honored, glorified, and extolled at the symbolic level and through embodied practice, and constitute social structural dominance over women as well as over other men. Indeed, hegemonic masculinities are constructed in relation to "complicit" masculinities (those that benefit from hegemony yet are not the "frontline troops" supporting dominance), to "subordinated" masculinities (based on race, class, age, and sexual preference, for example), and to "oppositional" masculinities (those that explicitly resist and possibly challenge hegemony). In fact, hegemonic masculinity is the dominant form of masculine gender practice in a given milieu in which other types of masculinities are complicit, subordinated, or opposed—not eliminated. For example, in the secondary school social setting, we are likely to find representations of hegemonic masculinities (e.g., "cool guys" and "jocks"), complicit masculinities (e.g., "regular guys"), subordinated masculinities (e.g., "gay boys," "wimps," and "nerds"), and oppositional masculinities (e.g., "freaks," "tough guys," and "profeminist boys"). Ethnographies of secondary schooling in Britain, Australia, and the United States consistently report such masculine power relationships (Connell 1996). The concept of hegemonic masculinity, then, identifies how particular boys and men exercise power over girls and women and other boys and men—historically and situationally (and therefore differently)—and how the gender relations that generate their dominance is legitimated and reproduced as well as challenged and changed. In short, gender practices are not equal because certain forms have more influence than others in particular settings.

Hegemonic masculinities and emphasized femininities, then, as the culturally and situationally dominant gender practices in particular settings, influence but do not determine masculine and feminine behavior. Hegemonic masculinities and emphasized femininities underpin the conventions applied in the enactment and reproduction of masculinities and femininities—the lived embodied patterns of meanings, which as they are experienced as practice, appear as reciprocally confirming.

As such, hegemonic masculinities and emphasized femininities shape a sense of reality for men and women in specific situations and are continually renewed, recreated, defended, and modified through practice. And yet they are at times resisted, limited, altered, and challenged. As Thorne (1993, 106) notes, "Individuals and groups develop varied forms of accommodation, reinterpretation, and resistance to ideologically hegemonic patterns." Consequently, hegemonic masculinities and emphasized femininities additionally operate as "on-hand" *discourses* (developed from embodied social actions themselves) available to be actualized into practice in a range of different circumstances. They provide a conceptual framework that is materialized in the design of social structures and, therefore, materialized in daily practices and interactions. At times and under certain social conditions men and women construct oppositional masculinities and femininities that in one way or another are extrinsic to and represent significant breaks from hegemonic and emphasized patterns, and may actually threaten their dominance. For example, such various oppositional practices as rebellion against authority and cross-gender practices (girls "doing" masculine practices and boys "doing" feminine practices) in secondary schools are constructed from specific social settings. Hegemonic and emphasized forms of gender practice are not merely adaptive and incorporative; authentic transgressions within and beyond them occur under specific social conditions.

The concepts of "hegemonic," "emphasized," "complicit," "subordinated," and "oppositional" masculinities and femininities permit investigation of the different ways men and women experience their everyday worlds from their particular positions in society and how they relate to other men and women. Although most men and women attempt to express some aspects of situationally practiced hegemonic masculinities and emphasized femininities through speech, dress, physical appearance, activities, and relationships with others, these embodied practices of masculinity and femininity are associated with the specific context of individual action and are for the most part self-regulated—often nonreflexively—within that context. Consequently, aspects of various masculinities and femininities can exist simultaneously. For example, a boy who rebels against authority in school (oppositional) may also engage in dominating and controlling practices of girls (hegemonic). This example of different gender strategies in action clearly reflects that masculinity and femininity are based on a social construct that mirrors unique circumstances and relationships—a social construction that is renegotiated in each particular context. In other words, social actors self-regulate their behavior and make specific choices in specific contexts. In this way, then, men and women construct varieties of gender through specific embodied practices. And by emphasizing diversity in masculine and feminine construction, we achieve a more fluid and situated approach to our understanding of embodied masculinities and violence.

EMBODIMENT

As I have emphasized, constructing gender entails embodied social practices—gendered structured action. Indeed, it is only through our bodies that we experience the social world, and the very possibility of a social world rests upon our embodiment (Crossley 2001). As Iris Marion Young (1990, 147–148) points out:

> It is the body in its orientation toward and action upon and within its surroundings that constitutes the initial meaning-given act. The body is the first locus of intentionality, as pure presence to the world and openness upon its possibilities. The most primordial intentional act is the motion of the body orienting itself with respect to and moving within its surroundings.

We understand the world from our embodied place in it and our perceptual awareness of situational surrounding space. The body is a sensuous being—it perceives, it touches, and it feels; it is a *lived body*. And given that consciousness consists of perceptual sensations, it is therefore part of the body and not a separate substance (Crossley 2001). The mind and the body are inseparably linked—a binary divide is a fiction—and live together as *one* in the social construction of gender. In this conceptualization, then, the body forms the whole of our being and, thus, one's "self" is located in the body, which in turn acts, and is acted upon, within a social environment. Indeed, in contemporary industrialized societies the body is central to the social construction of self (Giddens 1991). A proficient and able body is necessary for social action and, therefore, embodied discipline is fundamental to the competent social agent: "It is integral to the very nature both of agency and of being accepted (trusted) by others as competent" (Giddens 1991, 100).

Goffman's (1963, 1972, 1979) important work on behavior in public settings is relevant here, demonstrating how the body actually is the medium by which individuals become active participants in daily life. In particular, Goffman (1963) argues that situationally embodied forms of communication (what he calls "body idioms" and what have been labeled here as "gender practices") guide our perception of "appropriate" bodily appearances and behaviors and, therefore, serve as situational constraints. In this sense, then, *discourse* is not simply a free-floating force but, rather, bodies in our immediate social situations construct the knowledge we use to act in those situations. Meaning inheres in the explicit appearance and behavior of bodies, which are publicly available through our participation in social interaction. As Crossley (2001, 17) states: "We can only meet and interact with others in virtue of our embodiment, as meeting and interacting are sensuous acts, dependent both upon the sensory systems required to perceive others and the sensible qualities that allow one to be perceived—not to mention the motor capacities required for communication."

Discourse is quite simply embodied appearance and practice, including verbal communication. Through embodied social action, then, individuals do gender while simultaneously presenting gender practices as discourse for others as a consequence of their embodiment. As Nick Crossley states, the social situations in which embodied actions are oriented "are populated by others and it is these others, in part, towards whom the actions are oriented. Action is *other oriented*" (1995, 141). Embodied social action is "interwoven with the perceptual field of the agent," so that what we actually conceptualize are social situations that require specific "practical accommodation from our action"—we respect, acknowledge, reproduce, and sometimes resist situational embodied conventions (Crossley 1995, 136). And as Goffman (1979, 6) acutely observes, such embodied actions are situational forms of "social portraiture" in which individuals convey information that "the others in the gathering will need in order to manage their own courses of action—which knowledgeability he [sic] in turn must count on in carrying out his [sic] own designs." Doing gender therefore is necessarily both mindful and physical; it is intelligent and meaningful but it also involves "physical doings"—movement through space and physical engagement with other physical beings (Crossley 2001, 20).

Bodies then are active in the production and transmission of *intersubjective* gendered meanings, and embodied social actions "are executed in accordance with the others who populate the (intermundane) space of their exercise." In other words, embodied gender practices "are articulated with the behavior of others" (Crossley 1995, 146). Thus, the meaningfulness of our social action is based on the reaction of others to our embodiment—whether or not it is judged *accountable* is highly important to our sense of self. Embodied accountability is vital to an individual's situational recognition as a competent social agent. If an individual's embodied appearance and practice is categorized by others as "failed," that degradation may result in a spoiled self-concept (Goffman 1968). Consequently, adequate participation in social life depends upon the successful presenting, monitoring, and interpreting of bodies.

Goffman helps us understand how doing or practicing gender is intersubjective (because it is intercorporeal) in the sense that we accomplish gender *bodily* and in a manner that is acceptable to situationally populated others. Individuals exhibit embodied gender competence through their appearance and by producing situationally appropriate "behavioral styles" that respond properly to the styles produced by others. As Goffman (1979, 8) argues, "competent" individuals develop an embodied capacity "to provide and to read depictions of masculinity and femininity" in particular settings, and appropriate body management is crucial to the smooth flow of interaction essential to satisfactory attribution and accountability by others. Indeed, to be "read" by others as masculine or feminine, individuals must ensure that their proffered selves are maintained through situationally appropriate display and behavior—the body is social and social settings are created through intercorporeality.

But in addition, properly accountable bodies construct gender (as well as class, race, and sexual) relations; they signal and facilitate through their appearance and action the maintenance of gender power relations. To be sure, suitably adorned and comported bodies constitute the "shadow *and* the substance" of unequal gender relations (Goffman 1979, 6): "The expression of subordination and domination through the swarm of situational means is more than a mere tracing of symbol or ritualistic affirmation of social hierarchy. These expressions considerably constitute the hierarchy; they are the shadow *and* the substance." Individuals produce (and at times challenge) structured gender relations through their embodied appearance and actions.

Connell suggests that masculinity in particular is translated into "a certain feel to the skin, certain muscular shapes and tensions, certain postures and ways of moving, certain possibilities of sex." Thus, the physical sense of maleness is central to the social interpretation of gender (1995, 52–53). And hegemonic masculine embodiment usually occupies and controls space in particular settings. Indeed, gender difference and inequality is literally embodied in forms of carriage, demeanor, comportment, and the exercise of physicality over situational space. On the whole, for example, men and women sit, stand, gesture, and walk differently, and such difference constructs a seemingly "natural" inequality (Martin 1998; Young 1990). As Karin Martin (1998, 494) points out: "Generally, women's bodies are confined, their movements restricted. For example, women take smaller steps than men, sit in closed positions (arms and legs crossed across the body), take up less physical space than men, do not step, twist, or throw from the shoulder when throwing a ball, and are generally tentative when using their bodies."

Martin is describing the embodiment of emphasized femininity and, in this regard, Young maintains that such bodily practices have their root in the fact that women experience the body as "a mere thing" which exists as "looked at and acted upon." In contrast to hegemonic masculinity, then, for emphasized femininity "the body is often lived as a thing that is other than it, a thing like other things in the world" (1990, 150). To be sure, women's sense of self as "Other" develops bodily in constructing a fundamental gender project:

> The young girl acquires many subtle habits of feminine body comportment—
> walking like a girl, tilting her head like a girl, standing and sitting like a girl,

gesturing like a girl, and so on. The girl learns actively to hamper her movements. She is told that she must be careful not to get hurt, not to get dirty, not to tear her clothes, that the things she desires to do are dangerous for her. Thus she develops a bodily timidity that increases with age. In assuming herself to be a girl, she takes herself to be fragile. (Young 1990, 151)

Consequently, gender differences in bodily appearance and practice are socially "naturalized"—while natural similarities are suppressed and negated—and significant to reproducing gender inequality. As a wide variety of feminists have pointed out, in a patriarchal heterosexist culture the "male gaze" perpetuates such embodied inequalities. For example, Sandra Lee Bartky (1998, 34) notes that "a male connoisseur resides within the consciousness of most women: they stand perpetually before his gaze and under his judgment. Woman lives her body as seen by another, by a patriarchal Other."

Although departures from the above patterns clearly exist for both men and women—some of which are discussed in parts III and IV of this book—it is important to signify the distinct "lived bodies" of most (but not all) forms of hegemonic masculinity and emphasized femininity, and how such embodiment is embedded in, and often reproduces, unequal gender relations.

Thus, the body is an essential part of gender construction in which we fashion appearance and actions to create properly and situationally adorned and performed gendered bodies. This relationship between embodied discipline and gender is articulated interestingly in Harold Garfinkel's (1967, 118–140) discussion of the transsexual "Agnes," whose biological sex was male but who eventually adopted the self-attribution (and therefore the fundamental gender project) of a female. Garfinkel showed how gender is embodied through interaction and that accomplishing gender required persistent monitoring of the body and of bodily signs and practices. Garfinkel studied the embodied methods Agnes employed to "pass" as a "normal natural female" and how Agnes acquired a public "femaleness" by utilizing the appropriate "female" bodily skills, capacities, appearances, and practices. Garfinkel concluded that the study of such "violation cases" as Agnes demonstrated for us what we all do: the naturalness of the world in which there are two unequal sex categories is realized through conventional, self-regulated, often nonreflexive management of the body, and is an interactionally, intersubjective, and intercorporeal accomplished event. Thus, people "do" gender through embodied social action.

The body is an inescapable and integral part of doing gender, entailing social practice that "constantly refers to bodies and what bodies do, it is not social practice reduced to the body" (Connell 2000, 27). Constructing gender involves a dialectical relationship in which practice deals with the biological characteristics of bodies: "It gives them a social determination. The connection between social and natural structures is one of *practical relevance*, not causation" (Connell 1987, 78). Indeed, in the social construction of gender (as discussed in chapter 2), bodily similarities between men and women are negated and suppressed, whereas bodily differences are exaggerated. For example, early adolescent girls are generally physically bigger and stronger than boys their age, yet that bodily characteristic is subdued as enormous social pressure is applied to construct girls as dependent and fearful in comparison to boys (Connell 1987, 80).

Nevertheless, bodies participate in social action by delineating courses of social conduct: bodies are *agents* of social practice and, given the context, will do certain things and not others (Connell 2002a, 27). Indeed, our bodies constrain and facilitate social action and therefore mediate and influence social practices. The body is *lived* in terms of what it can "do" and, according to Connell, "[T]he consequence of bodily practice is historicity: the creation and transformation of situations. Bodies are drawn into history and history is constituted through bodies" (1998, 7). In short, the body is a participant in the shaping and generating of social practice. Consequently, it is impossible to consider human agency—and therefore crime and violence—without taking gendered embodiment into account.

CHALLENGES

Nevertheless, certain occasions present themselves as more effectively intimidating for demonstrating and affirming embodied masculinity and femininity. In certain situations individuals may experience body betrayal and be identified by others as embodying gender failure. The constitution of masculinity and femininity through bodily appearance and performance means that gender accountability is vulnerable when the situationally appropriate appearance and performance are not (for whatever reason) sustained. Because the taken-for-granted gender of individuals can be challenged in certain contexts, gender is particularly salient. It is, as David Morgan (1992, 47) puts it, "more or less explicitly put on the line," and the responding social action can generate a distinct type of gender construction. Such masculinity or femininity *challenges* are contextually embodied interactions that result in gender degradation—the individual is constructed as a "gender failed" member of society. Masculinity and femininity challenges arise from interactional threats and insults from peers, teachers, parents, workmates, and from situationally and bodily defined masculine and feminine expectations that are not achievable. Both, in various ways, proclaim a man or boy or a woman or girl subordinate in contextually defined masculine and/or feminine embodied terms.

Masculinity and femininity challenges may motivate social action toward specific situationally embodied gender practices (e.g., bullying and/or fighting) that *correct* the subordinating social situation, and various forms of crime and violence can be the result (Messerschmidt 1993, 1997, 2000). Given that such interactions question, undermine, and/or threaten one's masculinity or femininity, only contextually "appropriate" masculine or feminine embodied practices can help overcome the challenge. The existence of masculinity and femininity challenges alerts us to the transitory and fleeting nature of masculine and feminine construction, and to how crime and violence may arise as gender practices when masculinity or femininity are regularly threatened and contested.

Social action is never simply an autonomous event but is amalgamated into larger assemblages—what is labeled here as an embodied gender project. The situational ideals of hegemonic masculinity and emphasized femininity encourage specific lines of gendered action, and social structures shape the capacities from which gender projects are constructed over time. Men and boys and women and girls negotiate the situations that face them in everyday life, and in the process pursue a gender project. From this perspective, then, social action is often—but not always—designed with an eye to one's gender accountability individually, bodily, and situationally.

Structured action theory, then, permits us to transcend the mind–body, sex–gender, and gender difference binaries by conceptualizing masculinities and femininities more realistically and completely than power-control, strain, and other gender perspectives. Structured action theory enables us to explore how and in what respects masculine and feminine embodied practices are constituted in certain settings at certain times, and how embodied masculine and feminine practices relate to specifically interpersonal assaultive violence and nonviolence.

The study in which this theory is applied examines the construction and formation of masculine and feminine practices through violent or nonviolent social action as one aspect of certain individual embodied gender projects. Structured action theory is used to explore the ways adolescent-embodied masculine and feminine practices are constructed through interaction within the particular social context of home, school, and street. In short, to understand working-class adolescent violence and nonviolence, we must appreciate how structure and action are woven inextricably into the ongoing activities of "doing" embodied masculine and feminine practices.

• 4 •

A THEORIZED
LIFE HISTORY

This study investigates adolescent perpetrators of interpersonal assaultive violence in the context of their entire lives, from their earliest memories to the point at which I encountered them. Such life-history accounts lead to an understanding of the stages and critical periods in the processes of violent and nonviolent masculine and feminine development, and to an understanding of how the particular individual is both enabled and constrained by structural position. Criminology reports very little about the life histories of violent adolescent offenders and especially little about when, and under what type of social conditions, they may also be nonviolent. Although some recent criminological work contributes notably to our understanding of adolescent gender and crime (Archer 1995; Chesney-Lind and Hagedorn 1999; Chesney-Lind and Pasko 2004; Collison 1996; Hagedorn 1998; Joe-Laidler and Hunt 2001; Maher 1997; Messerschmidt 2000; Miller 2001), no life-history research on adolescent gendered violence exists and no studies on youth violence explore the similarities between boys and girls, or the role of the lived body, in the practice of assaultive violence or nonviolence.[1] Additionally, criminology historically has been haunted by (but has never addressed adequately) the question of why boys and girls who grow up simultaneously in the same or similar social milieu progress in different yet similar directions (assaultive violence) throughout the course of their lives.

The present study, then, seeks to understand certain boys' and girls' use of assaultive violence as a gendered practice. The chief questions of the study are: Why is it that some boys and girls engage in assaultive violence and how are these violent boys and girls similar and different? How are gender relations in specific settings—such as the family, the school, and the street—related to motivation for embodied violence and nonviolence by the same boys and girls? This differential use of assaultive violence is examined as a resource for "doing gender" in certain situations and under specific circumstances. To comprehend what it is about adolescent boys and girls that motivates some to commit assaultive violence, we must comprehend the social construction of gender—how assaultive violence may be a meaningful gendered construct and embodied practice in itself and in particular settings. To understand adolescent assaultive violence, then, we must bring actively gendered subjects solidly into the research picture.

The primary goal is to glean considerable and telling information from a modest sample of white working-class boys and girls who engaged in assaultive violence. By scrutinizing each detailed life history, we shall begin to learn the social processes involved in becoming violent or nonviolent in certain settings. I believe the study has several significant strengths. First, the boys and girls I interviewed reflect the serious (dark) end of the delinquent behavior continuum and represent a type of offender about whom criminologists must genuinely be concerned—assaultive adolescent males and females. Here *assaultive offenders* are boys and girls from fifteen to eighteen years of age who acted in a nonsexual physically violent way against at least one other person; there exists no official records of them committing any other type of violent act (e.g., homicide and/or rape) and they all denied engaging in any other type of violence, although they may have committed such other nonviolent crimes as property and drug offenses. Thus, in terms of violence, these boys and girls are exclusively assaultive offenders.[2]

Second, the study includes both boys and girls matched according to the following demographic characteristics:

- sex (male or female, as appropriate)
- age (15–18)
- social class (working class)
- race (white)
- contact physical violence (assault)
- age of victim (14–50)
- sex of victim (male or female)
- victim relationship (stranger, relative, or acquaintance)

Finally, the life-history method is particularly relevant because it richly documents personal choices, experiences, and transformations over time. A life history records "the relation between the social conditions that determine practice and the future social world that practice brings into being" (Connell 1995, 89). The life-history method is what William I. Thomas and Florian Znaniecki (1927) characterized as the "perfect" type of sociological material. Such classics of criminology as Clifford Shaw's (1930) *The Jack Roller*, Edwin Sutherland's (1937) *The Professional Thief*, and William Chambliss's (1972) *The Box Man* illustrate the "power of life-history data to illuminate the complex processes of criminal offending" (Sampson and Laub 1993, 203). Indeed, the life-history method is experiencing a resurgence in the social sciences, including the sociology of masculinities (Connell 1995; Messner 1992), the sociology of sexualities (Dowsett 1996), and the sociology of crime (Burman, Brown, and Batchelor 2001, 2003; Goetting 1999; Sampson and Laub 1993; Totten 2000). The resurgence is due in part to the fact that life histories tap continuous "lived experiences" of individuals. That is, the method demands a close evaluation of the meaning of social life for those who enact it—revealing their choices, experiences, embodied practices, and social world. As Terri Orbuch (1997, 455) points out in her important article "People's Accounts Count," the life history is significant sociologically because we gain "insight into human experience and arrive at meanings or culturally embedded normative explanations," insight that allows us to understand "the ways in which people organize views of themselves, of others, and of their social world." And Ken Plummer (2001, 242) eloquently summarized the value of life histories:

> To tell the story of a life may be at the heart of our cultures: connecting the inner world to the outer world, speaking to the subjective and the objective, establishing the boundaries of identities (of who one is and who one is not); crossing "brute being"—embodied and emotional—with "knowing self"—rational and irrational; making links across life phases and cohort generations; revealing historical shifts in a culture; establishing collective memories and imagined communities; telling of the concerns of their time and place.

Although individuals engage in violent and nonviolent embodied practices, this does not mean that everything about a person is accessible immediately to that person as well as to others—there is mystery. Yet the social process of becoming violent or nonviolent can be decoded by a reconstruction of the life history that relates later events to earlier choices, interactions, and practices (Connell 1987). Such life-history accounts are "destined to bring to light" the embodied practices by which an individual makes himself or herself a person (Sartre 1956, 734). As Robert Agnew (1990, 271) points out, these types of accounts of those involved in crime "may be the only way of obtaining accurate information on the individual's internal states and those aspects of the external situation that the individual is attending to."

In addition to in-depth documentation of an individual's social world and representations of choice, interaction, and embodied practice, the life history links the social and historical context in which both are embedded. As Bob Connell (1995, 89) points out, "The project that is documented in a life-history story is itself the relation between the social conditions that determine practice and the future social world that practice brings into being. That is to say, life-history method always concerns the making of social life through time. It is literally history."

Thus one salient feature of the life-history method in exploring assaultive violence by boys and girls is that it permits an in-depth understanding of the "interplay between structural fact and personal experience" (Connell 1991, 143). The life history can reveal what other methods can hide or obscure. The research here embraces a theorized life history as the specific method because the interviewing and interpretation are based on structured action theory (Connell 1991; Dowsett 1996). This particular procedure is "not a process of theorization by generalization, but a systematic method of investigating the operation of social processes through the recounted experiences of individual lives" (Dowsett 1996, 50).[3]

SAMPLE

Life-history research does not target large and representative samples from which to draw bold generalizations. Rather, in this study its goal is to uncover patterns and to provide useful cases that signal contributing factors to assaultive violence and nonviolence by white working-class adolescent boys and girls. Indeed, the sampling procedure can be best described as "stratified purposeful sampling" (Patton 1990, 172–174) to fit the theorized life-history method.

Ten white working-class adolescent boys and girls currently incarcerated, on probation, or undergoing private counseling for assaultive violence were selected to match the demographic variables identified earlier and then were categorized as "assaultive offender" (five boys and five girls). I chose these adolescents to avoid limiting the sample to boys and girls officially processed in the juvenile justice system. The incarcerated and on probation boys and girls were identified by prison personnel or juvenile probation officers who obtained the informed consent of each youth and their parents or guardians before I interviewed them. In private counseling the boys and girls were identified similarly by therapists prior to informed-consent interviews with me.

Additionally, I attempted to obtain a "mix" of youth from different family configurations (e.g., adoptive parents vs. biological parents; violent vs. nonviolent households).[4] This "maximum-variation" sampling procedure provided a selection of boys and girls from a wide range of home life and other background situations. The vast majority of the boys and girls simultaneously grew up in the same milieu (lived in the same neighborhood and attended the same school). The race and social class of the entire sample remained constant (white working class).

Some argue that we learn little from such a small sample. However, a detailed investigation of a few case studies often illuminates contributing factors concealed by other methodologies. Gary Dowsett (1996) points out that in other disciplines, such as the medical community, scholars frequently publish research based on a limited number of clinically observed cases. For example, a 1990 article published in the *American Journal of Public Health* documented:

> HIV seroconversions in gay men, related, it seems, exclusively to receptive oral intercourse with swallowed ejaculate. Given the ongoing unresolved debate about the likelihood of HIV transmission through oral-genital sex, this was a sensational finding. The article, however, was based on two cases, and although the authors' conclusions were properly cautionary, the example demonstrates that the chief concern need not always be the sampling method and sample size. (Dowsett 1996, 44)

Nevertheless, ten case studies is not a representative sample and, therefore, my conclusions—although properly cautionary—are illustrative and suggestive only. Notwithstanding the article just cited, the four life stories reported in part III (two boys and two girls) simultaneously show that important aspects of assaultive violence by white working-class teenagers have been overlooked and, therefore, present an extremely rich source for further investigation and theory building. As Solomin Kobrin (1982, 153) points out, life histories reveal the more "elusive elements of deviant behavior that are often difficult to capture in quantifiable variables." Each life story deepens and augments our understanding of the situational accomplishment of gender and of the eventual use of assaultive violence or nonviolence as a result of personal life history.

DATA COLLECTION

The theorized life-history method implemented here involved voluntary and confidential one-on-one tape-recorded "informal conversational interviews" (Patton 1990, 280–282). These conversations were conducted in private, secluded rooms and were completed in two meetings of three hours each. The conversations were fluid, allowing each boy and girl to take the lead rather than merely to respond to topical questions. The goal was to grasp each individual's unique viewpoint—his or her personal vision of the world. This interview method involved attempting to foster collaboration (rather than hierarchy) in the research process by judiciously engaging the boy or girl, "working interactionally to establish the discursive bases from which the respondent can articulate his or her relevant experiences" (Holstein and Gubrium 1995, 47).

This does not mean, however, that the conversations were unstructured. On the contrary, each conversation attempted to unearth the choices made, the situational interactions and accomplishment of embodied masculine and feminine practices, and the eventual use of violence and nonviolence in particular contexts and as a result of personal life history. As such, the interviews drew on the insights of structured action theory. I specifically sought detailed descriptions of choices and practices (what a boy or girl did, not solely how he or she felt) and accounts of interaction in families, peer and leisure groups, and schools. The conversations touched on intimate and sensitive areas of personal life and relationships. Topical examples I explored include (1) the division of labor between men and women in the adolescent's household and in the peer and leisure groups of which he or she is a member; (2) the power dynamics between male and female adults, between adults and children, among boys, among girls, and between boys and girls at school and in peer groups; (3) any masculine or feminine mentoring during childhood and adolescence; (4) his or her sexual awakening, how he or she managed it, and how images of sexuality were conveyed to him or her; (5) the meaning and practices of embodied masculinity and/or femininity and violence throughout his or her life course and how they were represented to him or her; (6) the tensions and conflicts in these processes and the way they changed over time; and (7) all gender challenges and violent events during each life course.

LIMITATIONS OF THE STUDY

Although life-history research provides rich areas of criminological knowledge, it is not without limitation. Indeed, there are traditional problems related to investigator effects; for example, the investigator recounts "only part of the story" (Short 1982, 135). However, as James Short responds, this criticism should not be seen as unique to life-history data: "Different methods tell different parts of a story and tell them differently" (1982, 135). As we know, all knowledge is partial and situated, derived in part from the researcher's authority and privilege (Richardson 1990). Life stories must be seen as active constructs in themselves, jointly developed by interviewer and interviewee. In critically assessing my place and position during each conversation, I followed suggestions of feminist sociologists that interviewers attempt to give up "authority over the people we study, but not the responsibility of authorship of our texts" (Reinhartz 1992, 28). This involved developing strategies to empower the interviewees during our interaction. For example, I met each adolescent twice, using the second conversation to carefully review together the content of the earlier conversation. This helped to break down hierarchy, to encourage the interviewees to find and speak the "correctness" of their stories, and to avoid treating each participant simply as an object of study.

Moreover, although all interviews are gendered contexts—whether they are single or mixed gender (this study involves both)—research suggests that "the gender of the interviewer is not an insurmountable barrier to establishing rapport and achieving reliable results in in-depth interviewing" (Williams and Heikes 1993, 289–290). Being especially concerned about interviewing across gender, class, and age (i.e., an adult middle-class man interviewing working-class teenage girls), I was encouraged to find that some studies comparing male and female researchers have established that the "definitions of the situation" conveyed by respondents (regardless of interviewer gender) show "remarkable similarity and overlap, even on topics involving gender and sexuality, which have been identified by survey researchers as the topics most sensitive to 'sex of interviewer effects'" (Williams and Heikes 1993, 289). Importantly, however, such a result is reached only by the researcher acknowledging from the outset that gender is an inevitable aspect of the research setting and by taking into account this inevitability in their research practice (Padfield and Procter 1996). Consequently, from the beginning of the research process I took steps to decrease gender as a salient issue during each interview. For example, I asked those obtaining the necessary informed consent (prison personnel, probation officers, and therapists) to ask each potential respondent if he or she had a "problem" talking with an adult man about intimate and possibly painful life experiences—not one boy or girl declined participation. Moreover, throughout our conversations I attempted to be mindful of gender construction and worked at minimizing hierarchy and maximizing collaboration and reciprocity. Following the suggestions of Margaret Andersen (1993) for "researching across difference," I did not present myself as an expert; I did not assume the passivity of respondents; and I did not force respondents to adapt to my definition of the interview situation. Rather, I emphasized how sincerely interested I was in learning about *their* lives from *their* points of view—I respected these adolescents as *experts* of their own life histories; I discussed with each interviewee selected aspects of my own life (including my experiences with violent victimization); and I enthusiastically answered any questions they posed to me. Moreover, I did not hide any emotions that developed out of heartrending accounts of certain events in their life stories. And my efforts seemed to have worked. At the end of the first interview respondents were asked if they would agree to a follow-up conversation—all but two boys agreed to a second interview, most with enthusiasm.[5] Additionally, the vast majority expressed excitement that I might include their life story in "a book." Overall, I believe that both the boys and the girls were trusting, open, and could have talked with me for many more hours than we shared. Although the adolescents I interviewed *may* report different things to a female interviewer, this does not make the life stories reported here any less salient and "honest." As Andersen points out: "If the task of sociology is to understand the multiple interactions between social structure and biographies, then the many ways in which we see ourselves and our relationships to others should be part of sociological accounts" (1993, 51).

The possibilities that respondents may, for example, lack memory of key events and/or issues or simply attempt to deceive the interviewer is an additional cautionary concern in life-history methodology. However, I agree with Robert Agnew's argument that there is no a priori reason to assume that boys and girls are more likely to be dishonest or subject to faulty memory during, for example, life-history interviews than they are when participating in such other procedures as self-report questionnaires and large-scale surveys. In each of these methodologies, answers to questions reflect the "respondents' perception of reality and events" (Agnew 1990, 269). Given that such "contaminants" may occur in any social science methodology, I chose to examine carefully what is expressed in each conversation and to treat each life history as a *situational truth*. As Ann Goetting (1999, 20) points out, life stories are not simply "true" representations of an objective "reality"; rather, the interpretations of both interviewer and interviewee "combine to create a particular view of reality."

Of necessity, I have built in research strategies that increase the credibility of findings. Prior to commencing an interview in a secluded room, I explained that risk of identification was negligible inasmuch as all interview information would be identified by a number only, stored in a secure facility, and destroyed by me at the conclusion of the study. Moreover, I pointed out that interview conversations would be treated with strict confidence, never made available to another person or agency, and that certain identifying details would be changed. Further, I obtained an informed consent prior to each interview. I also indicated that the final results of the research would be published in a manner that fully protected the interviewees' anonymity, family members, and all others mentioned during the interview. In addition, I addressed topics in different ways and at varying times during the interview. Interestingly, the answers rarely varied. Importantly, not only did I point out that our conversations would address issues that may be painful and stressful, I emphatically emphasized that each interviewee did not have to answer a question or talk about an issue if they chose not to. I consistently revisited the consent issue during our conversations, and underscored to each that he or she may stop taking part in the study at any time for any reason.[6]

Finally, in addition to joint construct, boys' and girls' accounts, like all interview data, probably are affected by meanings that are external to the conversation—such as what boys and girls learned in treatment and/or incarceration. Therefore, I specifically discussed with each respondent whether his or her responses were shaped by such experiences; that is, was his or her past behavior reinterpreted during our conversations in light of personal experiences in treatment, during incarceration, or while on probation. I consistently asked each respondent to recapture the past and respond as to how he or she conceptualized events at the time of enactment. In all cases, the boys and girls seemed able to distinguish what they learned in treatment and/or during incarceration about their behavior from what they felt in the past when the particular event occurred. Moreover, I discussed with therapists, counselors, and probation officers the nature of any treatment received by each boy and girl. For all participants in this study, gender was never a remedial part of their rehabilitation.

Although it is critical to verify factual information and consistency in storytelling, the primary task of the life-history researcher is not to establish an alleged "truth" but to describe—as stated earlier—how each particular life story assembles a specific situational truth. What is most critical is that the life story is "true" for the interviewee at that moment—that it captures an individual's personal reality and his or her unique definition of the situation. The aim is not simply to relate a particular life history to other cases in the project and to previous research findings (which I do), but to grasp each story for what it tells us about that specific case. In short, each conversation attempted to comprehend the revealed choices and embodied practices made during the respondent's life course, the formation of masculine and feminine practices, and the use of assaultive violence or nonviolence as outcomes of a personal trajectory constrained by his or her social structural position.

DATA ANALYSIS

Aware that there is "no such thing as an authentic experience unmediated by interpretation" and that "reaching conclusions in research is a social process and interpretation of data is always a 'political, contested and unstable activity'" (Burman, Batchelor, and Brown 2001, 454), my data analysis had two stages. First, tape-recorded conversations were transcribed and thoroughly analyzed, and individual case studies were prepared. Second, the life histories were dissected to define similarities and differences among the pathways to assaultive violence and nonviolence. Consistent with other theorized life-history methodology, the intent here is not simply to present biography but to explain social process through the life-history data (Connell 1995; Dowsett 1996).

The chapters that follow in part III attempt to capture each interviewee's embodied experience in his or her words. As such, I examine how individual social interaction with others is embedded in social structural constraints in particular settings. Moreover, by comparing individual life stories we can establish links among boys and among girls whose lives are quite different but who are affected by similar race and class position. In other words, we can discover the interconnections among boys and girls—as well as the differences and similarities between them—who live in a shared social context. Accordingly, theorized life-history methodology helps to register patterns in lives that other methodologies render invisible. And, as shown throughout chapters 5 and 6, there is much here to offer in our attempt to understand youth assaultive violence and nonviolence.

Finally, a brief note on the title of the book, *Flesh and Blood*. I chose it for two reasons. First, all the adolescents I interviewed who were involved in street groups referred to their peers as "family," and one assaultive girl actually described her street companions as "my flesh and blood." Thus, the title reflects this extension of its meaning beyond offspring or relatives. Second, metaphorically the term "flesh" refers to the body, and the concept "blood" to assaultive violence. In fact, one interviewee stated "you can only win a fight if you make 'em bleed," and another referred to his street group as "blood brothers." In short, the expression "flesh and blood" nicely highlights an expanded meaning of family and suitably conveys the notion of embodied assaultive violence.

PART III

ASSAULTIVE BOYS
AND GIRLS

• 5 •

WIMP AND BULLY

In the 1990s several school homicides occurred in the United States; nearly all the "school shooters" were boys (the single girl did not commit murder; see chapter 6) who had been bullied consistently, primarily concerning their bodily appearance, by bigger and stronger boys. For example, on October 1, 1997, in Pearl, Mississippi, Luke Woodham (aged sixteen) shot and killed two students in his high school. He was overweight, considered a "nerd," and often was called "pudgy" and "gay" at school by the athletic "cool guys." Two months later in West Paducah, Kentucky, Michael Carneal (aged fourteen) shot and killed three students in his junior high school. He was frequently bullied as a "wimp" by the "cool guys" at school—he was approximately five feet tall and weighed 110 pounds—and had been labeled "gay" in his school newspaper. And on April 20, 1999, in Littleton, Colorado, Eric Harris (aged eighteen) and Dylan Klebold (aged seventeen) shot and killed a teacher, twelve students, and themselves. They had been bullied routinely by "jocks" (e.g., shoved into lockers, pushed and slugged in the hallways, and ridiculed for their "looks") and were called numerous degrading names, including "faggot." All these school shooters were boys who embodied a subordinate masculinity in the context of school and, thus, "their violence was retaliatory against the threats to manhood" (Kimmel and Mahler 2003, 1439). Indeed, as Michael Carneal is reported to have stated: "I just wanted the guys to think I was cool. . . . People respect me now" (Kimmel and Mahler 2003, 1447).

Although none of the boys in this study were involved in school shootings, their life stories and the social processes surrounding their assaultive violence are similar to those of the killers just mentioned, from Pearl, Mississippi, to

Littleton, Colorado. Indeed, what the school shootings reveal are not simply the devastating consequences of peer verbal and physical abuse, but an oppressive hierarchically embodied relationship among boys that is institutionalized in schools. Like the boys involved in the school shootings, *all* the assaultive boys in this study were either socially categorized at school as "wimps" or "bullies." Logically, then, chapter 5 focuses on two white working-class boys involved in assaultive violence: Lenny and Perry (both pseudonyms). Lenny and Perry were chosen specifically from the larger pool of interviewees for three explicit reasons. First, Lenny was exclusively nonviolent at home whereas Perry occasionally engaged in assaultive violence in his home milieu. Thus, these two case studies facilitate comparison as to why boys may engage in violence or nonviolence in the family setting and how that particular embodied action is related to gender. Second, Lenny and Perry represent different embodied masculinities—"wimp" (Lenny) and "bully" (Perry)—and therefore typify two significantly different pathways into assaultive violence at school and on the street. Finally, these two case studies are nicely juxtaposed because both Lenny and Perry grew up in the same neighborhood and attended the same school at the same time. Accordingly, this chapter reports data as to why boys from the *same* social milieu engage in assaultive violence for *different* reasons and in the *different* settings of the home, the school, and the street. We begin in this chapter with Lenny.

LENNY

Lenny was a short, obese, and somewhat shy fifteen-year-old. He had short dark hair and wore blue jeans, a sweatshirt, and tennis shoes to each interview. He also wore a cap that was emblazoned "Give Blood, Play Hockey," yet he spoke to me in a skittish and soft-spoken manner. Although never formally charged or arrested for assaultive violence, at the time of the interviews Lenny was attending private counseling sessions for continually assaulting younger and smaller neighborhood boys. In what follows, I describe through Lenny's words his involvement in nonviolence at home and assaultive violence at school and on the street.

Nonviolence at Home

Lenny lived in a working-class neighborhood with his mother and father, an older brother (aged eighteen), and a younger sister (aged thirteen). The family lived in a two-bedroom upstairs apartment. Lenny had another brother (aged twenty-one) who did not live with the family. Lenny's earliest family memory is of the first time the family went camping: "We had a great time together, right by a lake, canoeing, hiking, roasting marshmallows and stuff."

Although both parents worked outside the home as unskilled laborers, the mother and sister were responsible for all domestic labor (the father did no domestic labor); they received only limited help from Lenny and his brother. Lenny and his brother shared a room; all three children were responsible for cleaning their respective rooms. This was not a problem because Lenny and his brother alternated cleaning the room they shared, and there seemed to be little quarrel regarding this. Lenny also reported a very warm and affectionate family environment: "My parents have a kinda family thing. We do things together. We go to beaches, camping, have cookouts, go to the movies. A lot of things I guess." However, Lenny mostly liked to do things with his father. Asked about his favorite activities, Lenny replied, "We go hunting each year—my father, my brothers, and me. My father bought me a 30/30. And I got my hunting license. My father helped me study to get my license. I studied with him. That was fun."

Asked further about hunting, Lenny said: "It's exciting to get ready 'cause we eat a big supper before and get up early and go. It's fun to be with my dad." I inquired about other activities Lenny did with his father, and he emphasized "fishing, swimming, catch, play darts. The whole family, we play board games; that's real fun."

Lenny's mother never disciplined Lenny and the other children. The father "took control" when he came home from work: "He never actually hit me, he just would get mad and talk serious to me. We didn't make him mad that much. We'd do what my dad and mom says."

At home, then, Lenny grew up under a conventional gender division of labor. Both parents performed "appropriate" gendered labor and other home-related activities—father embodied hegemonic masculinity; mother emphasized femininity. Although father was never physically violent, clearly he held the power in the family and used that power to control all decisions. For example, even when Lenny wanted to do something outside the home (e.g., go bike riding), he was not allowed to do it unless his father approved ahead of time. Lenny identified with his father—his initial model for developing an embodied conception of masculinity—engaging in accountably masculine appearance and practices (e.g., hunting, fishing, playing catch, etc.). Lenny thrived on his father's approval, such as when he shot his first deer ("Dad said he was real proud of me"), and conceptualized maleness as in part embracing the embodied practices of "working hard, being strong, a good hunter, and being like Dad." And given Lenny's

success at constructing such masculine appearance and practices—his fundamental gender project was to be "like Dad"—he never engaged in assaultive violence in the home milieu. Thus, Lenny embodied an accountably complicit—
yet simultaneously subordinate (through age)—masculine presence and *place* in
the in-home gender relations.

Violence at School and on the Street

Lenny did reasonably well in elementary and junior high school. For the most
part he liked his teachers and the schools, and he earned average grades. Most
recently, in eighth grade, he graduated with honors. For that he got a new bike:
"All my uncles and aunts, my mom and dad, they all pitched in and bought me
a[n] eighteen-speed. Pretty cool."

Nevertheless, at school Lenny received constant verbal abuse because of his
physical size and shape (shorter and heavier than the other boys and girls).
Other children call him a "slob," a "fat pig," and a "punk." Moreover, at school
kids continually abused him about his mother, whom they saw as extremely
obese: "Kids always say my mom is so fat, you know, and things like that. Kids
say that my mom is so stupid. They call her all kinds of names, and some swear
words—like she has a[n] elephant ass." Because of this peer abuse, Lenny developed a dislike of school: "I hated to go to school." When asked if he discussed
this abuse with his mother and father, Lenny replied: "My dad said that if somebody punches me, then I get the right to punch him back. If I'm being teased, I
tease him right back. Call him names back. If they [sic] teasing me always, then
my dad tells me that I should punch 'em back."

Lenny felt embarrassed at school because of his physical size and shape, and
because of his obese mother. Moreover, because he was smaller than the kids
abusing him, he felt insecure about responding as his father taught him. He
stated that the people abusing him were the "tough guys" in the school: "They
was the popular tough guys, and everyone laughed when I didn't do nothin'. I
couldn't. I felt really small in front of everybody."

Consequently, because of his embodied emasculation at school, Lenny became a loner and attempted to avoid the "tough guys." In addition, Lenny observed that other kids in school were being abused: some "would do nothin',
like me, and some would fight." It seems there were many school fights based on
verbal abuse. Lenny recalled the following example: "One time I was sitting
down by my locker and the big guys teased this kid. He [the abused boy] hit the
kid back, and he [the big guy] had a lot of friends, and they all jumped in on that
one kid." These types of events, then, led Lenny to become frightened of social

interaction at school; accordingly, he attempted to avoid school as much as possible. Indeed, there were fights in Lenny's school "about once every month"; apparently kids would fight about "everything." Lenny provided another example:

> Like one time a kid stole the other kid's comic cards. When he was in the hallway with them, the other kid came over and the kid gave 'em back but he beat him up 'cause he took 'em, over that. The kid gave 'em back to him, but he still beat him up. So I was always scared to talk to kids. I'd never know what might happen. So I went to school, went to my classes, and then ran home.

Q.: Are these tough kids looked up to in your school?
A.: Oh yeah. They are the neat kids. Everybody wanted to be tough like them.
Q.: You wanted to be tough like them, too?
A.: Yeah, I wanted to be like them.

Lenny wanted to be like the "tough guys" at school; he longed to go home and tell his father that he did not let anyone push him around at school. However, he was unable to embody masculinity as interaction with his father (and at school) had emphasized—which terrified him: "I couldn't tell my dad that I was afraid, 'cause then even him would call me a wimp, a scaredy-cat." By the time Lenny was fourteen, then, he lacked masculine bodily resources and thus felt extremely inferior at school—he failed to embody a masculine presence in this setting. Nevertheless, one school event provided an opportunity for Lenny to attempt masculinity as practiced by the other boys:

Q.: Tell me about that.
A.: There was this nerd of a kid that even I made fun of. He would wear high-waters.
Q.: What are high-waters?
A.: Kids that wear high pants.
Q.: Okay, go on.
A.: This high-water is real skinny and ugly. I'm bigger than him. So I go: "You look funny in those pants," and stuff like that. I called him a "nerd" and he said the same back to me. There was all these kids around, and so I beat him up in the hallway 'cause he called me a "nerd" and nobody liked him.
Q.: Why did you hit him?
A.: 'Cause he called me a name that I didn't like and I wasn't afraid of him.
Q.: What did other kids say who saw you beat him up?
A.: Some kids was happy 'cause nobody likes him. But some said I should pick on kids my own size. Plus I got ISS [in-school suspension].

Q.: Did you tell your dad about this fight?

A.: Yeah. I ran home and told him that this kid was making fun of me, so I beat him up and got ISS for it.

Q.: Did your father talk to the school officials about the fight?

A.: Nope. He was just happy I beat up the kid.

Q.: Is that the only fight in school?

A.: Yeah, 'cause he is the kid I can beat up at school. I can beat up kids in my neighborhood.

Lenny indicated that the assault of the "high-water" was his only school fight. He then provided detailed information about his involvement in neighborhood violence, the setting where his assaultive behavior concentrated. According to Lenny, numerous neighborhood boys would constantly challenge him to physical fights. However, he developed specific criteria for his participation in such challenges: "I fight if I can beat the kid. I got this kid next door, he calls me a 'fag.' I mean, there is no reason why he calls me a 'fag,' and my father said next time he does that 'beat him up.' My father says if I don't fight him, he'll [father] fight me. So I beat the kid up, and my father was happy."

Q.: Was this kid smaller than you?

A.: Oh yeah; I only fight kids I can beat up. My father says that's smart; you should only "pick the battles you can win."

Q.: How did it make you feel when you beat up neighborhood kids?

A.: It made me feel real good inside. I knew I wasn't a wimp anymore.

Q.: Did it bother you that the boys you beat up were smaller than you?

A.: No, 'cause of what my dad said. And I fought kids that called me names or said stuff about Mom.

Q.: Who are your friends?

A.: I don't have friends at school. Only kids in my neighborhood. I play with kids that are younger than me. We have fun together.

I discussed sexuality with Lenny. He told me he did not learn about sex from his parents but from "sex-ed" class at school. He also heard kids talking about sex with each other at school: "Some kids, even fourteen- and fifteen-year-olds, you know, are having sex in my school. And they talk about it, right out loud." Lenny never had a girlfriend or went on a date. However, occasionally he attended school dances and danced with several girls, but nothing ever developed. After the dance "I'd just go home." He asked girls for dates numerous times, but all refused. This bothered him somewhat because he wanted a girlfriend with whom to experience sexuality. He also wanted to have someone close with whom he could talk.

Q.: Did you ever feel you should have sex with girls?
A.: No.
Q.: Other kids were bragging about having sex, and did that make you feel you should also have sex to be cool?
A.: No, never. You don't have to have sex to be cool.

Lenny perceived himself as heterosexual without feeling that he had to "go out there and do it." If he had a girlfriend, he would like to experience sexuality because he was still a "virgin." However, Lenny pointed out that it did not bother him that he had not experienced sex: "It'll come someday." Although the "cool guys" were also the boys who publicly bragged about "getting laid," Lenny felt there existed numerous avenues to "being cool": "Some kids are cool because of the clothes they're wearing. Some kids smoke. Some are tough. Some play sports, roller-blading, biking. Not all cool kids have sex."

Lenny added that there were four major boy cliques in his school—the "jocks" (the tough and cool guys), the "nerds," the "smart kids," and the "losers." Although he felt he belonged to none of these groups, he believed that some of the "jocks" most likely considered him a "nerd" and a "wimp" because they always abused him—not only for his size and shape but also because he did not "fight back" and did not participate in any sport: "The jocks always teased the nerds and make fun of them for not playing sports." According to the "jocks," those (including Lenny) who did not play sports (especially football) and who did not retaliate in kind when bullied were "wimps" and "nerds." In fact, Lenny stated that "jocks" often called him a "wimp" because he did not play football and because he was not tough: "The jocks called me a wimp because they said I was afraid of gettin' tackled and afraid of fighting."

Q.: Did you feel you were a "wimp" and a "nerd"?
A.: Yeah, I did. I wanted to be tough like them, and I was tough to some kids.
Q.: How did it make you feel when you were tough with some kids?
A.: I didn't feel like I was a wimp anymore. I felt good. My dad said there's always someone bigger. And that goes for the big kids too. There are people who can beat them up.
Q.: What does it mean, then, to be a "real man"?
A.: To be tough, have muscles. Just big like my father, he's about six feet something. A good fighter like the guys at school.

Q.: Do you want to be a "real man"?

A.: Yeah! I want to get muscles because I want to be kinda strong in case people fight me. I want to be able to get them down, not to hurt them, but to get them down so they don't hurt me. I don't want them to fight me. I want to be strong enough to get them down.

I asked Lenny if there was anything else that he would include in his definition of a "real man." Surprisingly, he stated the following: "A real man is also a gentleman. That's a man. A man that don't hit girls. A man that hits girls is not a man."

Q.: Where did you learn that?

A.: From my father. My sister used to hit me, and I got really mad at her. I'd say, "I'm gonna punch you if you don't stop it." And my father says, "I don't think so." I threaten to punch her but my father says, "I don't think so."

Q.: Your father taught you not to hit girls?

A.: Yeah. He says boys should never hit girls. It's okay to hit boys but not girls. That's what he taught me.

Q.: Did your father ever hit your mother?

A.: Never.

When I asked Lenny whether there were gay and lesbian kids in his school, he stated that he did not know of any, but: "There is a gay person in my family. My brother, he's gay." Lenny's older brother (the twenty-one-year-old) is gay; his brother's sexual orientation seemed to be accepted by Lenny's family: "Yeah, my family don't care. He comes over to my house. My family likes him. We had a cookout with him and his boyfriend. We all had a great time."

Q.: So you know the difference between heterosexuality and homosexuality?

A.: Of course.

Q.: Should you be heterosexual to be a "real man"?

A.: What? My brother is a real man. He's tall like my father and he lifts weights in his basement, so he's strong. He bikes and jogs and stuff. And he could fight if he wanted.

Lenny grew up in a nonviolent household that emphasized family cooperation and stability as well as sexual diversity and being a "gentleman" toward women; Lenny never engaged in assaultive violence at home. Notwithstanding, his father emphasized, as masculine criteria, male power in the home and "fighting back" against consistently verbally abusive males. Given that Lenny was often verbally abused at school for his physical size and shape, and for not being "a man," he accepted the notion that being masculine meant responding to provocation with physical violence—although because he was physically small and obese in relation to the bullies, he was unable generally to respond in such a "manly" fashion. Although Lenny embodied masculine presence and was accountably complicit at home, at school he was essentially emasculated.

Nevertheless, Lenny wanted to satisfy his father's criteria as well as be like the tough guys at school—he wanted to "do" hegemonic masculinity as defined both at home and at school. Consequently, Lenny felt comfortable verbally abusing a "high-water." When the "high-water" retaliated verbally, Lenny understood through the embodied discourses at home and at school that he was permitted then to assault him publicly at school. Because this did not completely work out as planned—numerous students having criticized him for not picking on someone his own size—he failed to embody a masculine presence at school and thus he concentrated his assaultive violence on his neighborhood. If the smaller and younger neighborhood boys verbally abused him, Lenny willingly fought them in the street setting. Thus Lenny practiced embodied masculine power over a few neighborhood boys through assaultive violence. This in turn gave him a sense of masculine self-esteem—he became hegemonically and accountably masculine in the street setting—because of the favorable appraisal he received from, in particular, his father. Nevertheless, eventually Lenny's assaultive violence on the street "got out-of-hand" and a neighborhood parent contacted the police. To avoid a formal charge of assault, Lenny (following the recommendation of the police and his parents) agreed to obtain private counseling.

PERRY

Perry had the physical appearance that many revere in teenage boys—he was tall, dark, muscular, and handsome. He presented a calm and cool persona, and his direct and self-assured style suggested greater sophistication than most seventeen-year-olds possess. Perry wore a bright-blue youth-prison "jump suit" and tennis shoes during each interview; he was serving a sentence for aggravated assault and numerous property and drug offenses. What follows is Perry's account of engaging in assaultive violence in all three settings of home, school, and street.

Violence at Home

Perry's earliest family memory was of his biological parents' constant arguing. Their conflictual relationship increased when his father lost his job. "Money problems" became an issue, and subsequently both parents became heavy drinkers. Each quarrel ended with Perry's father physically assaulting his mother. When Perry was four years old, his parents divorced and Perry lived alone with his mother, never seeing his father again.

Following the divorce, living with mother was fun for Perry because she stopped drinking and began to "spoil" him by providing money and toys when he wanted; she did not require that he perform any household chores. Perry recounted one of his most memorable activities with his mother: "On her days off and on the weekends, it was like a tradition to go out and eat and go shopping, to go and see relatives. Every Sunday we'd go and see my grandmother, and we would go out to eat and visit for a while."

Perry's mom worked full-time in the unskilled service sector of the economy, and he always looked forward to her coming home from work. Perry had a very close relationship with his mother and found it "really easy to talk to her about things." Whenever he experienced problems, he indicated that "[I]t felt good to talk to [his] mom about it." When Perry misbehaved, his mother always sat down with him and they both talked it out—there never was yelling or corporal punishment.

When Perry was seven years old, his mother remarried and his life changed dramatically: "The stepfather was real nice to me when they were dating, but when he came into the house he kind of laid down the law. He was the authority figure, and I didn't always get what I wanted." Perry's stepfather "had all the power. . . . My mom didn't really have any say in anything that went on in the house." Moreover, the stepfather brought his two children (ages two and four) to live with Perry and his mother.

At first Perry was "really excited" about having a younger brother and sister. However, his stepfather always seemed touchy and quick-tempered when Perry was around his new siblings: "Like I get yelled at and screamed at for the littlest things I did, you know, like laughing at a TV show while my brother and sister are sleeping. He gave me this "gung-ho" attitude. He was real strict. I got grounded all the time."

Perry's stepfather would not let him "hang out" with certain friends. He received an allowance (if he did his chores) instead of money when he wanted it. And Perry was required to "do the dishes, vacuum all the rooms, pick up messes, and stuff like that. Plus, homework had to be done right after I got home

from school." Overall, Perry saw his stepfather as a distant and uncaring patriarchal presence who did very little around the house: "My mom and me did all the
cleaning and stuff."

A lot of the arguments between Perry and his stepfather began when his stepfather came home from work (he worked in the skilled labor market): "If he'd
had a bad day at work he would just come up and start saying stuff to me, and I
would say something back, and then the argument usually would lead to something real physical—like he'd throw me around. He was never really like that to
my mother, brother, and sister—never."

Because his stepfather was in a "bad mood" three or four times a week, there
were frequent verbal and physical confrontations between the two. Thus
Perry's early models of masculinity (both his biological father and his stepfather) emphasized male power in the home as a masculine characteristic. Additionally, his stepfather's physically violent response to disagreements validated
interpersonal violence as an appropriate embodied masculine method of solving problems. Thus, at home the stepfather embodied hegemonic masculinity,
the mother emphasized femininity, and Perry embodied a subordinate masculinity.

Despite his troubled home life, Perry had many neighborhood friends with
whom he spent considerable time playing: "I was always out with all my friends
playing football, basketball, and we'd get real big organized games going on.
They were like my second family." Perry spent as much time as possible with his
friends, because it was fun and he "didn't see [his] stepfather."

Perry loved sports when growing up, and had visions of playing in the National Football League. Interested in all sports, he especially liked football. He
was a starting lineman on the junior-high football team and did much better
schoolwork during football season. Moreover, his room was filled with "sports
stuff": "My room was loaded. I had football posters on my ceiling, on my walls,
on my door. I had a basketball hoop that was a big net to hold my dirty clothes.
I had everything, football lamps, you name it."

Perry was very close to his uncle: "When my stepfather and my mother got
married, my uncle was kind of like a father figure. He'd take me out of the house
and stuff. We did a lot of things that my stepfather wouldn't do for me."

Q.: What kinds of things did you do with your uncle?
A.: Play basketball, play football, and do all the things my stepfather didn't do.
He'd take me fishing. He'd take me out to eat, buy me clothes, buy me toys.
He'd take me out of the house as much as he could. He was a really great
guy.

Q.: You liked to spend time with your uncle?

A.: Yeah. It was a good thing to see him, and I felt real close to him. I really cared about him. And he liked me. He always said I was good at sports, a natural. That made me feel good inside.

Q.: Did you learn anything special from your uncle?

A.: He was the one that first got me started thinking about sex. He had these ornaments, car fresheners, and I always used to laugh at them, you know, being naked women on the front of it. And he'd say, "Do you have girlfriends?" And I'd say "No," that I wasn't really interested in girls. And then he would tell me all about sex. He talked a lot about it. He didn't tell me to use rubbers and stuff. He just told me about getting a hard-on and what you do with girls, and that I would like to do it with girls. We made bets on it.

Q.: What were the bets?

A.: On when I would get laid. How old I would be.

Q.: Did you ever talk to your mother or stepfather about sex?

A.: My mom never said a thing. My stepfather just was always reminding me when I was going somewhere to have a rubber. If I was going to go screw girls or going to meet girls.

Q.: That's all he said?

A.: That's it. But my uncle talked to me a lot about sex.

Perry and his uncle also discussed the ongoing distressful relationship with his stepfather. He told his uncle how his stepfather hit him and pushed him around the house.

Q.: What did your uncle say?

A.: He said he knew about that, and that he and my stepfather got into a fight a couple of times over him hitting me. That made me feel good. I felt that someone cared. My mother never stood up for me, but my uncle did.

Q.: Were you unable to talk with your mother?

A.: More and more my mom started to side with my stepfather. They both yelled at me all the time. When he came into the house, my mom and me was not close anymore.

Q.: When your uncle stood up for you did that teach you anything?

A.: I got the impression from my uncle getting into fights with my stepfather that it was the right thing to do. Doing this kind of thing was the right thing 'cause I saw this guy that [I] really looked up to doing that.

Q.: He taught you about violence?

A.: Yeah, of course. If someone's fucking with you or fucking with someone close to you, you kick their ass. I learned that from my uncle.

Q.: Was your uncle an important model in your life?

A.: Yeah. He was a great guy. I wanted to be like him 'cause he didn't put up with any shit from anybody.

Primarily because of this encouragement from his uncle—and also because of the overall masculine discourse at home supporting masculine violence—early in the fall of his seventh-grade year Perry physically fought with his stepfather; he had grown considerably bigger and, as he states, "I wanted to show him like my uncle did."

> I was upstairs in my room listening to some rap music rather loud, and he came in and said he couldn't hear himself think. So I went to turn my stereo down and he kicked a hole in my speaker. I was like, "What the hell did you do that for? Why did you have to be an asshole?" Then he just turned around and snickered and punched me in the face. And I pushed him into my stereo system, and it fell down and a big rack fell on top of him. And he got up, busted my stereo, destroyed all my CDs, and I ran downstairs to the kitchen. He chased me and I grabbed a knife and held it up to him, and I was like, "Hey, back off." He rushed me. I knocked him to the floor and then ran to a friend's house. The cops came and arrested me—not my stepfather.

Being larger physically gave Perry the confidence to stand up against his stepfather—he now embodied an oppositional masculinity at home. And it felt good finally to retaliate physically. For quite some time Perry had wanted to "hit" his stepfather—especially after learning from his close mentor (his uncle) that such a response was legitimate and preferred—but he had always been relatively small. Now, as Perry put it, "I was bigger, and it felt good to knock him down. It was my turn to get physical and I did and it felt real good."

Violence at School and on the Street

In school Perry did reasonably well through sixth grade: "I was getting As and Bs, doing really good in my classes, getting really good comments from my teachers, and that really felt good inside." Perry liked his teachers, felt comfortable talking to them, and enjoyed school. He had many friends, and loved participating in organized school sports. Through sixth grade, then, Perry remained nonviolent at school.

In the seventh grade, however, Perry began getting into trouble. Sometimes he would "fool around" in class by hassling other students, and teachers as well. As Perry stated, "I kind of lived for showing off in front of my friends. You know, we would kind of show off in front of each other, and we kind of lived for that." Asked what he did in class to "show off," Perry stated he would: "smack a kid in the face or steal his books or misplace something of his, rip up his homework. I would make some kid in class look like a fool, you know. Everybody in the class would be laughing, and I felt good about that."

Perry engaged in this type of conduct up through the eighth grade: "I was constantly getting suspended from school. My stepfather didn't like that and was getting more angry." Indeed, Perry attributes "home life" as primarily causing his changed attitude toward school. That is, because Perry could now physically respond to a more powerful stepfather, in turn he felt comfortable making "a fool" of "wimps" by bullying them. Eventually Perry used his "growth spurt" to justify frequent fights at school. A typical fight scenario was as follows: "Most of the time it was a kid who would get real mouthy and get cocky, and he would have this real tough-guy attitude. I usually started by hitting these little wimps, trying to look tough—where I was the biggest—and usually the fights stopped right there. I'd start and finish it."

For his behavior, Perry gained the status of "school bully"—he now embodied an exemplary masculine presence at school. "Usually not too many people would come my way looking for trouble, but if they did they were trying to prove something. They were trying to get my status. But they got their ass kicked instead."

Q.: Other kids looked up to you?
A.: Yeah. I was a football player and the school bully. People jumped when I moved. Everyone wanted to be my friend.
Q.: Were there different cliques in your school?
A.: Yeah. There was the smart kids. There was the quiet, ugly, and dumb kids who everyone looked down on 'cause they was wimps. And there was us, the athletes, party animals.
Q.: Were you a "cool guy" in school?
A.: In some ways. In my friends' eyes. The real "cool guys" was the smart ones that played sports. We played sports, partied, and kicked ass. Everyone was afraid of us.
Q.: Did you and your friends talk about sex?
A.: Yeah. Like who had the biggest breasts, who was the loosest, who gave the best head, who screwed the best.

Q.: Was having sex important to you and your friends?

A.: Of course. All my friends got laid all the time. And I remember when they said, "We're going to get Perry a fuck tonight."

Q.: Tell me about that experience.

A.: My first experience was at a party. There was this friend—a really good friend of mine—and he'd have these big parties and have a lot of girls at his house, and everybody would be getting something. So I was thirteen years old, and I had gone to this party. And I was already drinking and doing all that stuff, and doing drugs. And it kinda surprised me. I found out after that my friend sent this girl over and we started to fool around with each other, and then the situation kinda having us getting the groove on, you know. And that was the first time I ever had sex.

After this first sexual experience, Perry frequently engaged in intercourse. Indeed, it was a major part of his group interaction at school and his form of embodied masculinity. Although the teachers did not know of Perry's sexual exploits, he was suspended from school after each physical fight, and when he returned to school he would almost immediately get into another fight. Ultimately, he assaulted teachers as well. Once he attacked a teacher because "He was trying to intimidate me. He was getting in my face, giving me glances." Perry was suspended for that assault; eventually he was expelled (but not formally arrested or charged) for the following incident:

> I was like being vulgar to the teacher, and when he got mad I told him to "suck it." And he told me to get out of class. And once out in the hall he cornered me and started yelling at me. Once he got too close I just like smashed him, and he kind of like bounced off the wall and kind of fell down. And that's when three or four teachers grabbed me and brought me up to the office.

Q.: Did you like any of your teachers?

A.: No. They were always trying to lay down the law. I didn't like them in my face, trying to confront me.

Q.: What did your classmates think of your behavior in class?

A.: I gained status in front of other kids when I didn't put up with it. They wished they could do the same but couldn't, so they looked up to me.

Throughout his seventh and eighth grades, then, Perry defined masculinity against the school and its overall project. He enjoyed a tough reputation and the masculine status it earned. Accordingly, he constructed an in-school opposition masculinity.

At age fourteen and toward the end of his eighth-grade year, Perry was expelled from school (never to return); immediately after expulsion his uncle died. The following is an extended dialogue of how this event—in conjunction with other circumstances—was a major turning point in Perry's life.

> When my uncle died I lost it for a long time. I didn't want to come out of my room. I just kinda wanted to be by myself. I couldn't get it through my head that he was dead and I couldn't picture him not being there for me—to be able to talk to, to be able to have him pick me up and do things with.

Q.: Did your mother comfort you?

A.: A little. But she was on my stepfather's side 'cause I got expelled. So she just gave up on me and defended my stepfather all the time.

Q.: How did your stepfather respond to the death of your uncle?

A.: He said he was sorry that my uncle died "But you've got chores to do." It was like that. I hated him for that, and so I ran away.

Q.: You ran away from home?

A.: Why stay? My uncle was dead. My mom sided with my stepfather. I hated my stepfather. And I was kicked out of school. I hated what was going on around me, so I just left and I'm glad I did.

Q.: Where did you go when you ran away?

A.: I went and stayed with friends at their house. Their parents would let me stay.

Q.: Did you go to school?

A.: No. I was expelled and they wouldn't let me back in. If my friends decided to go to school, I'd just hang out on the streets. I'd go and find ways to make money—like break into cars, break into stores, and people's houses.

Q.: Why did you do that?

A.: I needed some money, plus it was an adrenaline rush. Breaking into houses really got my adrenaline pumping, and then to run from the house and not get caught. It was fun 'cause I always got some cash and I always felt good about myself while I was doing it.

Q.: Why did that feel good?

A.: 'Cause I got away for [with] it. And the people I lived with did it. And we all laughed about how easy it was. We didn't have to work for a thing.

Q.: Did you always do that alone?

A.: At first alone. But then a lot of my friends started dropping out, and we would all hang together, get money to get drugs, get fried, and get some food.

Q.: What kind of crimes did you commit?

A.: Mostly breaking into cars and houses, and stealing cars. We would take all we could get our hands on. Houses was the most fun 'cause, you know, it was exciting to be in someone's house and go through all their shit. If we happened to be doing drugs at the time we broke into a house, we'd had the munchies and we'd go right for the refrigerator and help ourselves. At the time we really weren't worried about getting caught by the police, because we had like a flawless record, you know. We'd break into houses and we'd never get in trouble for it. We figured, hey, break into a house, get something to eat, take anything we'd want, and get out.

After being expelled from school, only three things were important to Perry and his friends: "getting laid, getting hammered, and getting fried. It all had to do with drugs, alcohol, and sex. It was just those three things." They sold what they stole to a local fence, using the money to rent an apartment, buy food, clothes, drugs, and alcohol.

Indeed, feeling disconnected from home and school, Perry was attracted to the "street life" because he was "getting something from the drugs and the alcohol and the sex that [he] wasn't getting from school and books—and that was a feeling inside." I asked Perry to describe that feeling for me: "It was the 'rush,' the freedom to do what I wanted to do with my friends. I didn't have my stepfather telling me what to do, and teachers or principals telling me what to do. And I had people who cared for me. Like I said, we was like a family."

Perry did not characterize the people he hung out with as a "gang" but rather as "just a group of friends who liked to hang out. We just kinda stuck together and just did things." There were no special "uniforms" or requirements to join this group:

> The only thing you had to be in our group of friends was that you had to be there for each other. If someone needed back in a fight and someone needed some help with money or something like that, you'd be there to help them out. You didn't have to get beaten up by all of these people to get in our group of people. You didn't have to go do something to get in with our group of people. You just had to be a good guy, you know—a friend.

Q.: Were there girls in your group?

A.: Yeah. Some.

Q.: Did they participate in the same crimes as the boys?

A.: Yeah, sometimes. There was some girls that stole from stores and stuff. But mostly they just hang out and get hammered, get fried, and have sex with us.

Q.: Was sex important to everyone in the group?

A.: Oh yeah. We had like a competition. We would see how many girls we could screw in one week and how many nuts [orgasms] we could bust in one day.

Q.: Is it ever appropriate to have sex with a girl if she does not want to?

A.: Of course not. I heard of guys raping girls—but not my friends. We didn't need to 'cause the girls that hung out always wanted it, you know. That's what they lived for, you know.

Q.: Were there "boyfriends" and "girlfriends" in your group?

A.: No. We was just one happy family and we always meeting new girls, you know.

Q.: What about homosexuality?

A.: We didn't approve of it. As a matter of fact, we beat homosexuals up.

Q.: Give me an example of that.

A.: A bunch of them was having this big barbecue. And we went down there. We had already been drinking. We had a big van full of people, and my friend said, "Oh, look at all the faggots down there." And we all thought that was pretty funny. And then my friend said: "Let's go down there and beat some ass, go beat them faggots." And I was like "alright." So there were six or seven of us in the van, so we all went down and just started making fun of them. And one of the faggots told us to get the fuck away from them, and I went up to him and said, "Oh, you talking shit. You don't tell me to get the fuck out of here." And then I beat the shit out of him. It was fun until the cops came and we got arrested.

Q.: Why did you assault that person?

A.: 'Cause he was talking shit, and nobody talks shit to me.

Q.: Do you engage in violence whenever someone "talks shit" to you?

A.: When someone challenges me. When someone tries to intimidate me. When they get up in my face or if they hint that they want to fight me. If they get physical with me, I'm gonna get physical back.

Q.: Did girls in your group fight?

A.: No, they never did. That's one of the ways we see as being masculine. Girls are not aggressive and don't fight.

Q.: What did you see as masculine when you were in the eighth grade?

A.: Being tough, being good at sports, and having lots of people respect you.

Q.: How about after being expelled from school?

A.: Having courage to do things—like who had the biggest balls, who had the most courage. If you had balls enough to go and break into a house or steal a car, then you were something else. And being masculine was screwing the most girls, who could fight the best, who had the courage to do certain things, like I said, who could hold the most beer, smoke the most weed.

Perry learned at home and at school that physical violence was an appropriate and accountable response to masculine threat. Indeed, such conduct defined the character of his mentor and subsequently of his masculinity; Perry constructed practices at home, at school, and on the street that reproduced that masculinity. He moved from a subordinate to an oppositional masculine presence at home; Perry used his physicality to protect himself against a physically violent stepfather. And in school and on the street, he dominated others by embodying situationally specific forms of oppositional masculinity (at school) and hegemonic masculinity (on the street). Predictably, Perry responded with assaultive violence when others challenged his masculinity, eventually being arrested and convicted for assaulting a gay man and for various property and drug offenses.

• 6 •

BADASS AND LADYBUG

As I mentioned at the beginning of chapter 5, a number of school homicides occurred in the United States in the 1990s, all of which were committed by boys. However, one "school shooter" who did *not* commit murder was fourteen-year-old Elizabeth Bush. On March 7, 2001, in Williamsport, Pennsylvania, Elizabeth brought her father's handgun to school and shot a popular cheerleader captain in the shoulder. Elizabeth had been told consistently by this cheerleader and other "cool girls" at school that she was "fat," "ugly," and a "gay social misfit." The "cool girls" often pushed Elizabeth around and threw stones at her as she walked home from school. And these same girls knocked her books on the floor when they passed her desk and kicked her school locker door when Elizabeth was using it. To a certain extent, then, this school shooting is similar to the school shootings by boys who likewise were bullied about their bodily appearance and actions. However, the particular case of Elizabeth Bush is different from the boy "school shooters" in the sense that Elizabeth was also identified in her junior high school as a protector of "underdogs." Numerous racial minority students in her school were bullied (e.g., notes with racist slurs were passed on to them) by the "cool kids," and Elizabeth publicly protected them on several occasions. Thus, Elizabeth was bullied and rejected by the "cool girls" for her bodily appearance and actions—she was an in-school "nerd" who, additionally, befriended and attempted to protect other ostracized students.

Although none of the girls in the present study were involved in school shootings, the events surrounding their assaultive violence are similar to what occurred in Williamsport, Pennsylvania. Indeed, like the school shootings by boys, Elizabeth

Bush's case reveals not simply verbal and physical peer abuse, but an oppressive hierarchically embodied relationship among girls that is institutionalized in schools. However, as we will see in this chapter, there also are significant differences between assaultive violence performed by boys and by girls. Thus, I focus here on the life story of two white adolescent working-class girls involved in assaultive violence: Tina and Kelly (both pseudonyms). To allow adequate comparison with Lenny and Perry, Tina and Kelly were chosen specifically from the larger pool of interviewees for three reasons that paralleled choosing Lenny and Perry. First, Tina engaged in assaultive violence at home; Kelly was nonviolent at home. As with Lenny and Perry, I compare why these girls engaged in violence/nonviolence in the family setting and how that particular embodied action is related to gender. Second, Tina and Kelly embodied gender differently at school and on the street—Tina constructed a bad-girl femininity that occasionally involved assaultive violence (at home and at school but not on the street); Kelly constructed a stable masculine gender project that frequently involved assaultive violence at both school and on the street but not at home. These two girls then typify two significantly different pathways into assaultive violence and nonviolence in the three settings of home, school, and street. Finally, the two case studies are appealing because like Lenny and Perry, Tina and Kelly grew up in the same neighborhood and attended the same school at the same time. This chapter likewise reports data as to why girls from the *same* social milieu engage in assaultive violence for *different* reasons and in *different* settings (the family, the school, and the street). We begin with Tina.

TINA

Tina is a tall, slim, eighteen-year-old who has shoulder-length blonde hair. To each interview she wore considerable makeup, close fitting pants, a tight crop top, and numerous pieces of jewelry on her ears, wrists, and neck—she resembles Britney Spears in physicality and gender appearance. Nevertheless, Tina did not become a pop star singer but, rather, she became a "badass" and she currently is on juvenile probation for an assault that occurred at school. Let's examine how this transpired by contrasting the period in her life when she was nonviolent to the period when she was violent.

Nonviolence

For most of her childhood Tina lived with her mother and her stepfather (she is an only child). Tina's mother worked full-time as a nurse's aide and her stepfather worked as a day laborer "who took jobs here and there." Tina has no memory of her biological father but she does recollect a "life of hell" in her family. As Tina pointed out, her stepfather was "very abusive. I [used] to watch him beat Mom when I was little. He'd physically attack her and verbally abuse her." The battering of Tina's mother was constant—"It was always going on." And, not surprisingly, the stepfather "basically did nothin' around the house." As Tina continued, "Mom and me did everything, you know. She'd come from workin' all day at the hospital, and then fix food and clean up. He just sat there. And she was always doing stuff on her day off, like laundry and stuff. I'd help out what I could." Thus, Tina found herself living in structured gender relations at home that were constituted by a patriarchal division of labor and power—stepfather embodied hegemonic masculinity, and mother emphasized femininity.

Tina had a very close and nurturing relationship with her mother—"Mom and me have always been like real good friends; we talk about everything and help each other out"—who encouraged femininity by teaching her, as Tina put it, "to be a perfect girl. She taught me all the girl stuff, you know." And because of their affectionate and warm relationship, Tina engaged in accountably emphasized feminine display and practices at home (e.g., hairstyle, attire, and taking responsibility for the domestic labor). In addition, Tina wanted to do something about her stepfather's violence—"I wanted to stop this guy, you know, 'cause Mom didn't deserve what was happening to her." However, Tina could not stop the battering because of her physical size. During her early childhood, Tina was short and skinny and, therefore, she felt intimidated by and frightened of her stepfather. Although her mother was much bigger and stronger, Tina recognized that she was unable to defend herself against her abusive partner—"All she did is scream and cry, she couldn't fight back." In fact, Tina emphasized a deep concern about her mother's physical and verbal powerlessness numerous times during our conversations, most likely because she and her mother had a mutually supportive relationship. For example, when the stepfather battered her mother, Tina would scream and cry in an attempt to "protect Mom." Similarly, in verbal confrontations between Tina and her stepfather, mother often would intervene, which commonly resulted "in a beating for Mom." Such acts of reciprocal protection were accompanied by emotional support and comfort following each attack and, therefore, this mother–daughter relationship-strengthening interaction constituted accountably feminine practices at home. Moreover, by age ten—as a part of Tina's emotional support for her mother—she frequently would communicate the following: "Leave him. Leave him. He's an asshole. He doesn't treat you right." Tina's mother responded that she was too physically frightened to leave him. Consequently, because of her physical size and commitment to protecting her mother, Tina appropriated and embodied emphasized feminine nonviolent methods to stop the stepfather's violence: "I'd talk to him. I'd scream at him. I'd cry. And none stopped him from abusing Mom. It just got worse."

Through grade six, Tina was a model student: She earned "straight As," got along well with teachers, diligently did her homework everyday, and had many friends. Tina was also a popular practicing member of the "preppy" group. As Tina states: "I was with the preppies up to grade six. We had competition with each other, you know, like who could get the best grades. And I'd usually win." Tina added: "I was a real cute girl too, with lots of boyfriends." Tina considered herself a "cute girl" because she was "slim and good looking," she wore "the right clothes," and she had "lotsa 'puppy loves' with the cute guys" at school. In fact, there existed only three things the preppy girls cared about: "good grades, how we looked, and boyfriends."

I asked Tina to describe the structure of girls' groups in her middle school. She stated that there existed "a whole bunch of different groups of girls." The groups were small (on average about five girls per group), and her group was the most popular—the touchstone of emphasized femininity in the school. Other than her preppy group there existed various "jock" groups as well as a "badass" girl group, but there were also many girls in groups that were not easily identified—"just girls being friends, that's all"—and girls involved in several groups simultaneously (i.e., preppy and jocks). Thus, Tina described a relationship in which girls often moved from group to group, sometimes having intricate connections to several groups at once. However, there were two groups with clearly defined boundaries in a hierarchical relationship—the "preppies" and the "badasses"—and it was not easy to be accepted into either group. These two groups defined the major gender relations among girls at school—the preppies, of course, represented emphasized femininity; the badasses exemplified an oppositional femininity.

Entering elementary school, then, the structure of girls' groups presented Tina with some constraints and possibilities of where to position herself "as a girl"—she embodied a specific *place* in the gender relations of the school—and Tina helped reproduce the structure by becoming an accountable, practicing member of the most popular preppy group. Indeed, through grade six, Tina developed a controlled and cooperative gender strategy of action for institutional success at school. Tina's gender agenda simply was to become an accomplice to the gender order of the school and its intact gender relations among girls—in which she succeeded—and she never engaged in physical violence at school (or at home) during this time period.

Assaultive Violence

Despite Tina's nonviolent attempts to protect her mother at home through crying, talking, and screaming, her stepfather's violence continued unabated until Tina was twelve years old. By this age Tina—like Perry—had experienced a "growth spurt" and was now taller than her stepfather. Consequently, Tina decided she could help protect her mother in a different way—a physical way. Tina described the first such interaction with her stepfather as follows:

> They had this king size bed, and I was laying on it watching Mom put her makeup on when she was getting ready to go to work. My stepfather came in and told Mom he wanted breakfast. She didn't say anything, so I told him, "No way," you know, that she was busy gettin' ready for work. He should like make his own damn breakfast. I [used] to be intimidated by him but I wasn't anymore. And then he goes, "You get my breakfast ready or I'm gonna beat the shit out of you," like that. And then I just jumped on him and started hitting him in the face. That's when I just started really protecting Mom.

I asked Tina how she hit him and she responded, "I just like jumped on him and then slugged him in the face with my fist, just like he did to Mom."

Tina then felt comfortable physically challenging her stepfather because, as she put it, "I was bigger than him and I just had enough of his shit, you know, the way he treated Mom. And Mom didn't do shit, you know. So I had to do somethin' to stop him." Tina's stepfather did not retaliate by physically hitting Tina with his fists (as he did to her mother). Instead, "He just got my arms real hard and then he'd slam me on the floor. I'd get bruises on my arms and where I hit the floor." Tina's mother "always thanked [her] for doing that" but simultaneously she urged Tina "over and over again" to refrain from physically hitting her stepfather because "you'll really get hurt one of these times." But Tina responded to her mother that "somethin' had to be done"—and that "somethin'" was assaultive violence. As Tina expressed it, "I learned that for myself from my stepfather, how to hit, you know. I'd hit him like he hit Mom. He'd hit Mom to get her to do things for him, you know. So I thought I would hit him too so he'd stop hitting Mom, to protect her, you know."

At age twelve, then, Tina changed from a verbal (emphasized femininity) to a physical protector (oppositional femininity), and used assaultive violence to safeguard her mother from stepfather violence. During the year she turned twelve, Tina had approximately twenty similar physical encounters with her stepfather; that is, whenever he attempted "to go after Mom, you know, if it looked like he was going to beat on her, I'd be there. I'd just jump on him and start hitting him." Tina's stepfather frequently would verbalize, "If you keep tryin' to protect her, I'm gonna beat the shit out of you too." But according to Tina, "he didn't [beat her], he'd just throw me around, so I'd keep going after him." And Tina soon realized that her assaultive violence was successful: "Once I started reacting to him and I got better using my fists, he kinda backed down. He wouldn't throw me around as much and didn't hit Mom as much. And once I hit him and cut him on the forehead and there was blood all over the place, we hardly saw him around the house." In fact, soon after the forehead injury her stepfather actually moved out of the house. In answer to the question of how her stepfather's violence impacted her, Tina stated: "It made me stronger. I kinda felt powerful, you know, 'cause it made me stronger against him. I wanted to protect Mom, so I had to be stronger than Mom in a way when it came to my stepfather. I had to be strong like my stepfather, and it worked."

Tina also expressed that assaultive violence is not something "only men do. Girls do it too. And Mom should of a long time ago. But she couldn't, so I did. You know, it was just somethin' I had to do." Tina's commitment to assaultive violence against her stepfather to protect her mother not only helped rid the family of oppression, it also had an empowering impact on Tina. And when I asked Tina how her mother responded to this "success" she stated: "I'd never seen Mom so happy. She still thinks it's cool that I kicked that asshole out of the house." The end result of Tina's assaultive violence at home was not simply her embodied self-empowerment, then, but a reinforced close bond between mother and daughter.

Other than the assaultive violence toward her stepfather, throughout the first twelve years of her life Tina strictly engaged in emphasized feminine bodily display at home—"I always wore girl kinda clothes and even started wearing makeup around [age] ten"—and she happily helped her mother with such domestic labor as cooking food, cleaning up after meals, doing the laundry, and vacuuming. As Tina states: "I liked doing those things and I wanted to help Mom. I always liked dressing and acting like a girl, you know, so I did." And following her stepfather's departure, Tina never again engaged in assaultive violence at home.

Tina's emphasized femininity at school was likewise upset at the beginning of the seventh grade when she assaulted her best friend. During the summer just prior to entering the seventh grade, Tina began to dress in a more sexually provocative manner than she had earlier—"I'd wear real tight pants, lotsa makeup, high heels, stuff like that. It was kind of a experiment, I guess. I wanted to see if I could look better, and I did. So I would keep dressin' that way." Tina stated that part of her reason to "look better" was formed by reading specific "girl magazines" that influenced to a certain extent her choice of clothing, makeup, and hairstyle. However, the most significant influence on her were the "badass girls" at school who seemed to have "lotsa boyfriends"; she wanted to have "lotsa boyfriends" as well. As Tina stated: "And it worked. The guys liked the way I dressed and looked."

Tina physically retaliated against her best friend because she "told me I dressed like a whore, you know. She kept saying it over and over again. So I knocked her ass back with my fists and kicked her, just like I did my stepfather." This fight occurred "right in the hallway. It was real quick so we didn't get suspended." I asked Tina specifically what was bothersome about the above statement by her best friend, and she replied: "'Cause it was from like my best friend, you know. She'd never said that before and she kept sayin' it. And it made me feel like I didn't look right, you know, 'cause I thought I looked great and so did the guys. I liked the 'new me,' you know. So it like really bothered me. So I put a stop to it." In addition, Tina responded with assaultive violence because her "toughness" with an abusive stepfather led her to realize that she could likewise use her new bodily skill to fight back against such verbal abuse at school.

Because of Tina's fight with her best friend, the preppy girls subsequently rejected her as a member of their group: "They would like talk about me behind my back. Make fun of me, like call me a tomboy and stuff because I beat her up. Write nasty notes and say stuff to me in the hallways, you know." Tina thus experienced peer interaction that accentuated the impropriety of her gender appearance and assaultive violence as a girl. Tina responded, "It bothered me that my best friends kinda kicked me out, you know, 'cause I really liked them. But when they started to call me names and stuff, I decided no way, you know. I just don't want to be like them, they're stupid."

Although Tina was banished from the preppy group, she was praised for fighting by numerous girls at school, especially those associated with the badass group. Indeed, because of her fighting ability and her suggestive gender appearance, Tina was recruited into—as she now puts it—the "wrong crowd." She was attracted to the badass group because these particular girls "are hot looking and didn't act all catty and stuff. They didn't just say shit about people and like giggle around guys, you know, like the preppies; they partied with them." Tina started drinking alcohol with some badass girls, and occasionally would "sneak out" from home and "hang with my new friends." Tina particularly liked this group because "They dressed cool, looked good, and didn't take shit, didn't act stupid like preppy girls. So I wanted to be accepted by them. They saw me fight, and the way I looked, and it was kind of a 'get back,' you know, at my preppy friends." Tina joined the badass group to "get back" at the preppy girls and, because she was simultaneously "hot looking" and could "intimidate people," they accepted her. Tina described further: "I got adrenaline out of it. I thought I was cool. It was cool to sneak out at midnight, only twelve years old. Drinking, dress up hot, partying with guys. I thought this is cool, you know. We're *bad*, you know. It gave me a feeling of power." Tina felt powerful because she was now "doin' things preppy girls wouldn't do and showin' that we're *bad*, you know. That was power." The badass girls would "skip school a lot, smoke cigarettes, dope, and just kinda walk around, you know, get all dressed up and go to the mall. I thought it was the cool thing to do." Thus, the badass group maintained an embodied appearance and actions that were appealing and inviting to Tina. She adds that being a member of this group nicely coalesced with her newly acquired ability to fight, and this combination gave her additional feelings of power: "I felt more powerful, you know. I could fight them [preppy girls]. I'd go after them if they talk shit about me. So they wouldn't say nothin' in the hallways, you know."

Having learned at home that physical intimidation and aggression are legitimate avenues for gaining power, it is not surprising that Tina utilized this embodied practice at school as well—especially because the badass group in the peer school structure correspondingly authorized such practices *for girls* under certain conditions. Indeed, according to Tina, although the badass boys were involved much more often than the badass girls (and the preppy boys) in assaultive violence at school, and in more serious types of violence, both the badass girls *and* boys thought it appropriate for girls to fight girls "'cause you can't let people stomp all over you." Tina's former preppy friends verbally abused her less often because, as Tina states, "I'm 'badass,' I'm a *bad* girl, man. That's the way they saw me now." Tina developed a "Don't-mess-with-me" embodied reputation at school because of her now "tough" persona. She described her new in-school gender practices as follows: "Just go up to preppies and give them a look, you know. And say, 'What you lookin' at?' and 'You talkin' shit?' Stuff like that. And then they'd say 'No' and like run away." Because Tina was now taller than most of the preppy girls, height gave her confidence to not "take any shit from them or my stepfather. Plus I was known as crazy—as *bad*—you know, so people didn't mess with me." Tina characterized "crazy" as being "*bad*: just sneakin' out and hangin' out with my friends until late at night, you know, takin' people [preppy girls] down that talk shit. That's how I got the reputation. Just doin' crazy stuff that preppy girls are afraid to do or can't do." From her point of view, then, Tina raised her in-school status—she embodied a new *place* in the in-school gender relations—through her physical ability to intimidate preppy girls. In short, Tina maintained an oppositional bad-girl feminine presence at school.

Tina's new group of girlfriends were badass in the sense of skipping school, drinking alcohol, smoking cigarettes and marijuana, dressing in exaggerated feminine display, partying and having sex with boys, and physically intimidating and sometimes fighting preppy girls (never boys or other girls) at school. Tina fought only preppy girls at school because "Other girls don't give me shit, only the preppies." This left me curious as to why Tina never fought boys at school, especially given the fact that she had successfully and literally kicked her stepfather out of the house. Her response was: "I would [fight] if a guy gave me shit and I thought I could take him down, you know. Or if my boyfriend tried to slap me around, I would." But Tina never experienced such interaction with boys or her boyfriend(s), "So I never got in fights with guys." Tina also pointed out that none of the girls she "hung with" fought guys, "But that's because our guy friends and boyfriends never give us shit, 'cause they'd know what would happen if they did."

As an accountable member of the badass group, then, Tina would "dress up in like cute shorts or a short skirt or tight pants, high heels, dress up my hair, get tanned and stuff, and intimidate people, fight preppy girls, party, and look for cute guys." Tina explained why she chose the specific style of dress she did: "A girl has to present herself good, you know. If you have it, you have to show you have it. It gives you confidence to show it, you know. And I have it so I show it, and guys like it!" In other words, Tina combined "being bad" with strikingly conspicuous displays and practices of femininity at school.

Tina also provided examples of her participation in fighting at school. She emphasized again that she only fought preppy girls, and she was specific as to the particular circumstances that would motivate her aggression:

Once I fought this preppy girl 'cause she said I look like a whore. She was talkin' shit about the way I dressed and stuff, like my best friend, so I kicked her ass bad. I'd been in lotsa fights with preppy girls who'd be tryin' to give me shit about the way I act, callin' me a tomboy or a slut and stuff, so I beat them up. I just fight preppy girls who'd be mostly talkin' shit about me, you know.

When Tina fought preppy girls she would "hit 'em hard with my fists and kick sometimes, you know. But I mostly hit. Learned that from my stepfather." I asked Tina if she and the badass girls were attempting to be like boys when they fought. She responded: "Shit no. We fight like guys but we aren't guys. We ain't no tomboys. We're girls who don't take any shit from the preppies, you know. Girls fight too."

Thus, in the short span of one school year (seventh grade), Tina developed a specific badass persona and presence at school that distinguished and protected her from preppy girls who would "talk shit." Being *bad* required demonstrating to badass girls and boys not only that she was "hot," but also her actual capacity for effective physical violence when victimized by preppy girl verbal-peer abuse.

Tina indicated that the badass girls would "now and then hang out" on the street with the "badass boys," whom she described as "really *bad*, you know, fucking up all kinds of people, stompin', robberies, burglaries. All kinds of shit." Although Tina never participated in any of this criminal activity—"They [the boys] wouldn't let us if we wanted"—the badass girls "would chill with them. We'd party with them. Drink, smoke dope and stuff, you know." I asked Tina if she would participate in "stomping" (group violence) with these boys. Her response was that she "just partied with them. We'd never stomp with them, that's what guys do. They wouldn't let us if we wanted—but we never wanted." Thus, Tina embodied a badass form of emphasized femininity in relation to the badass boys. Although this gender division of conduct and power existed regarding badass criminal activities, Tina indicated that the badass boys "liked" when she and the other girls fought preppy girls at school: "They'd call it 'cat fights,' that it was fun to watch, and they'd always say we was good not taking any shit from preppy girls, you know, 'cause they didn't like the preppies either." However, Tina was nonviolent on the street.

Several of Tina's boyfriends were members of this badass boy group, and both badass girls and boys considered heterosexual monogamy the ideal. However, if a badass girl is "unattached," then it is acceptable for her to be promiscuous: "We had sex with lotsa guys if we didn't have a boyfriend, you know. We'd party and have lotsa fun with guys."

Tina became heterosexually active at age twelve and became pregnant at age fifteen. She immediately obtained an abortion, "'Cause there is no way I could take care of a baby." The pregnancy and the abortion eventually motivated Tina's final in-school fight, which occurred on the first day of high school (ninth grade):

> The first day of my freshman year this preppy girl called me a "slut." And then I beat the living shit out of her. Twice. For two days in a row. I said to her, "Are you talkin' shit?" "You callin' me a 'slut'?" And before she could answer, bam, I knocked her down, you know. The second time was at the school bus stop to go home from school the next day. I beat the living shit out of her there too. I ain't no slut and I showed her that. I got suspended for four weeks. I said, "Fuck it. I'm not going back." So I didn't.

Tina had been called a "slut" numerous times at school by preppy girls— only when she was "unattached" or pregnant—and she always responded with assaultive violence. Along with her suspension Tina was arrested—because the victim's parents pressed charges—and eventually convicted, and she is now on probation for that assault.

Navigating the gender relations among girl groups in her school, Tina initially became an accountable member of the most popular group and embodied emphasized femininity. However, conflict with this group arose when Tina engaged in what the preppies deemed inappropriate feminine behavior: Tina "beat up" her best friend and began to display herself in a sexually provocative manner. Accepting her rejection from the preppy group, Tina changed her place in the in-school gender relations and found social support for such behavior in the badass girl group, embodying an oppositional bad-girl femininity that entailed a combination of "being bad" (occasionally physically intimidating and fighting preppy girls and an overall tough persona) and exaggerated feminine displays (in terms of attire, hairstyle, and makeup) and practices (such as heterosexual promiscuity). In other words, as a now-accountable member of the badass group at school and on the street, during certain types of interaction exclusively at school assaultive violence was an acceptable practice. Although maintaining a publicly visible "Don't-mess-with-me" embodied capacity for violence, because Tina was rarely in a situation to experience a femininity challenge on the street, she—like the other badass girls—was nonviolent and thus embodied a badass emphasized femininity in this setting. As at home, then, Tina appropriated and rejected certain practices of copresent interactants in the two milieus of school and street.

KELLY

Kelly is a short, stocky, seventeen-year-old who eloquently presented her life history. At each interview she met me without makeup, with her shoulder-length blonde hair always pulled back in a ponytail, and wearing the same worker boots, baggy jeans, and sweatshirt with a hood. Kelly currently is on probation for an assaultive conviction. What follows is a close look at Kelly's development of practicing nonviolence at home yet engaging in assaultive violence at school and on the street.

Nonviolence at Home

Kelly's earliest childhood memory is when her youngest sister was born; Kelly was three at the time. The birth impacted her because she was no longer "the baby" of the family and no longer received the attention she had in the past. Nevertheless, Kelly's mother comforted her by stating that now having three daughters was like having cookies and cream: "I was the cream and my two sisters were the cookies." That is the last "nice thing" Kelly remembers her mother ever saying to her.

Kelly lived with her biological mother, a stepfather (she never met her biological father), a younger sister (by three years), and an older sister (by four years). Her stepfather was a factory worker and her mother "just stayed at home." When I asked Kelly if her mother was a homemaker, she responded: "Yeah, if that's what you call it. A drunken homemaker!" Although Kelly's mother occasionally would clean parts of the house, do some of the laundry, and cook a few family meals, she spent most of her daily hours "drinking alcohol and watching TV." The only household labor Kelly's stepfather did was taking the trash to the town dump, building household furniture, and "keeping his cars and snowmobiles running." As such, Kelly grew up among an explicit gender division of household labor. In addition, Kelly's stepfather was physically and verbally abusive to Kelly's mother. As Kelly put it:

> My stepfather would come home from work, like every night, and start to yell and beat on my Mom. She was always drunk and hardly did what he wanted, like clean and have dinner ready. So he would yell at her for that, you know, and she'd try to block him but she couldn't. She was too weak. He'd hit her, punch her, kick her, throw her all over the house.

Like Tina, then, Kelly grew up confronting patriarchal relations at home in which the stepfather (hegemonic masculinity) frequently wielded power through physical and verbal abuse over the mother (emphasized femininity).

The family never did anything together "as a whole family," as it was divided profoundly between mother and sisters on the one side and Kelly and her stepfather on the other side. Because her mother was either occupied with her younger sister or "too drunk" to interact with her (and her older sister was away from home "as much as possible"), Kelly spent most of her time with her stepfather. Kelly had turned to her stepfather for warmth and affection, and considered him to be her primary parent because they did "everything" together: "We played around with cars, played games, built furniture and stuff, and worked on his cars and snowmobile." Kelly's stepfather ignored all other members of the family—except when physically and verbally abusing them—yet engaged in "quality time" with Kelly: "He would tuck me in at night. He would let me sit on his lap when we watched TV. He'd give me hugs and kisses good night. He'd carry me on his shoulders. He'd give me piggyback rides. And he'd twirl me around with my hands. And I was the only one who got to go riding the snowmobile with him. He basically ignored my sisters."

Although he practiced a violent and physically powerful hegemonic masculinity, Kelly became extremely attached to her stepfather. This mutual affection and devotion between Kelly and her stepfather provided an escape from her overtly oppressive environment: Kelly consciously adopted what her stepfather practiced. That is, Kelly appropriated his type of masculinity as her own, rather than the femininity of her mother or her older sister. Consider the following response when I asked Kelly what she learned from her stepfather: "He'd teach me guy stuff, you know. He kinda made me into a tomboy, I guess you could say. He always said that he didn't have any boys of his own so he wanted me to be the boy. And I kinda really liked it." Kelly's stepfather did not "make" her into a "tomboy" but, rather, the gender relations and overall interaction at home led Kelly to embody an accountably complicit masculinity. For example, one aspect of "doing masculinity" in the family that Kelly relished was practicing certain gendered privileges. Kelly explains how the special bond with her stepfather empowered her to embody such privileges:

> I could be messy and my sisters couldn't. And they had to keep their room clean and I didn't. They had to do dishes and help my Mom with stuff. I could just throw my clothes on the floor and they couldn't. Oh, and when we were eating dinner in front of the TV, it was only my stepfather and me. My sisters and mom had to eat at the kitchen table. And I'd like just watch him, you know. When he'd be finished he'd just throw his plate to the side and he'd look at me and he'd go like, "You can, go ahead." And I'd throw my plate to the side like he did.

Kelly's stepfather ordered her older sister and mother to pick up after Kelly. The two never protested because "If they did, he'd come down on them. My sister hated me for that, and I think my Mom did too."

Although Kelly had no desire to work in a factory like her stepfather, she nevertheless wanted to do what he did because they seemed to be the "fun things." Kelly's stepfather taught her how to ride a dirt bike, a four-wheeler, and a snowmobile. The two watched sports together, such as the New England Patriots football games on TV, and "We tossed the football around alot." Neither sister engaged in these types of bodily practices and interaction with their stepfather.

Confronting patriarchal gender relations at home, then, Kelly understood the advantages and benefits of being "Daddy's boy," as this allowed her, for example, to "be messy," to avoid domestic labor, and to escape the repercussions of

her stepfather's physical and verbal abuse. Accordingly, Kelly became accountably masculine—"I just decided I didn't want to act like a girl, it was more fun to
act boyish" and thereby occupied a unique *place* in the in-home gender relations. Thus, a principal requirement of her complicit masculinity entailed distancing herself from all that is feminine. In fact, Kelly "hated" to dress and act
like a girl. For example, she disliked dresses because they made it difficult to play
sports, climb trees, and they would inevitably become "all torn up by the end of
the day from playing outside with boys." Eventually her mother stopped pres-
suring her to "dress like a girl," and she has since worn baggy jeans, work boots,
sweatshirts, and occasionally a duckbill hat. Kelly thought it made life easier to
dress "like a boy" and it was "more fun to act like a boy because I could do anything I wanted. My stepfather even taught me that it was okay to burp out loud.
He taught me how to make a mess and that it was okay to fart out loud whenever
I wanted." Kelly thus embodied masculine display and practices—including certain bodily emissions—and distanced herself from the femininity of her mother
and sisters because:

> They would always be wearing clean clothes and making sure they look okay and
> that [their faces are flawless]. My mother and my sisters have to wear dresses, cook
> for people, clean up, and stuff like that. Who wants to do that shit? It was just stu-
> pid. Girls are wimps. They aren't very strong. They do boring stuff, and they're
> afraid of everything. They hear a noise and they are like—ah, you know. It's just
> stupid.

I asked Kelly if her mother was a role model for her in any way. She responded:

> Not at all. She would kiss my boo-boos but I didn't want to end up like her, you
> know. She just has like a real boring life, you know. She's a fucking drunk and she
> just let my stepfather like push her around. She'd always do what he told her or
> she'd get beat up and there wasn't nothin' she could do about it. What kinda life
> is that? I did what my stepfather did 'cause it was fun to do guy stuff, you know,
> and I looked up to him.[1]

Rejecting femininity and embodying masculinity also provided Kelly power
through violence. For example, when I asked Kelly whether it bothered her that
her stepfather physically abused her mother, she responded that her mother
"had it comin', 'cause she always hassled my stepfather, you know. She got what
she deserved." Kelly defined her mother as a "hassle" to her stepfather because
she "just got drunk all the time, give him shit, not do anything around the house,

just lazy, you know." In contrast, Kelly looked up to her stepfather because "[h]e taught me all kinds of things and he didn't take no shit from my mom. So that had a lot of influence on me, you know. My mom didn't really care about me, you know, but my stepfather did." Despite this endorsement of violence and her embodied masculine presence, Kelly never engaged in assaultive violence at home.

Violence at School and on the Street

Through sixth grade Kelly enjoyed school, had a few friends, got along well with teachers, and maintained a C average. Kelly considered that she and her friends (mostly boys) were the "jocks" at school who never did anything wrong and had great fun together playing sports on the playground. Given that Tina and Kelly—like Lenny and Perry—attended the same school at the same time, Kelly described the structure of girls' groups at school in an identical manner as Tina—the "preppies" and the "badass"—and a variety of not-so-distinct girl groups. The preppies were the most popular girl group. The "jocks" were not organized into a specific group, they "just played sports together." As Kelly notes, "Us jocks hung out with all kinds of people."

However, in the seventh grade Kelly became a loner because her friends had suddenly rejected her. And often she was the victim of peer abuse: "I would get bullied, mostly by the jocks, for the clothes I would wear and because I shaved the back of my head. My clothes weren't up to fashion and they started to call me names 'cause I looked like a boy, you know, and acted like a boy. So I'd get picked on about that. And my old friends would always be talking behind my back."

Kelly explained that she wore "boys clothes" because "[i]t was easier to do boy stuff and I didn't want to look like a girl, you know." Kelly also shaved the back of her head and wore a duck-bill sports hat to further enhance her effort to avoid "looking like a girl." Kelly's friends did not have a problem with her overall "boyish" embodiment, but when she shaved the back of her head they began to reject her, and the girls in particular talked behind her back: "They'd stare at me and then whisper stuff to each other. Then they'd walk by me and call me a 'dyke,' and then they'd all laugh. And once someone drew a picture of me looking like a guy with a big dick, and they put it on my gym locker." Kelly was also subjected to peer abuse by boys who often called her a "wimp," told her that she simply "was a fucking girl," and bellowed at her to "stop acting like a guy 'cause you can't do guy stuff." Thus, Kelly experienced peer interaction that accentuated the impropriety of her embodied display and practices as a girl and as a boy. In short, Kelly was deemed doubly deviant at school.

Because Kelly was the sole female "jock" who dressed in such a manner, she attributed her peers' perception of her shaved head as "going too far for them." I asked Kelly how she responded to this development:

It really bothered me for awhile that my old girl friends turned against me. I felt confused and didn't know what to do. So I stopped playing sports 'cause I didn't want to be around them, I didn't want to be called names, you know. But after a while I knew that they just wanted to be popular, you know. And I hated the popular preppy girls. All they care about is their faces, their ass, and boys. They're wimps and they just do all this boring stuff. My old girl friends just wanted to be like them and I didn't.[2]

What especially and continually concerned Kelly was peer abuse by the boys, particularly being told she was a "wimp," allegedly unfit to do "guy stuff." As Kelly stated: "That really bothered me the most, 'cause I didn't like being hassled, but I couldn't fight like guys do. I kinda felt like a wimp when guys would like hassle me, you know, about that." Because of her physical size—Kelly was shorter than most of the boys who verbally abused her—she lacked confidence in "fighting back," as the masculine culture of the school dictated. Consequently, Kelly talked with her stepfather about the peer abuse at school, "And he said I needed to threaten the boys, you know. To go after the boys, not the girls, so everyone can see me, you know. To do it so kids could see. Like, 'You keep it up and I'll take you down.' And then when they [boys and girls] saw what I did to a couple of guys at school they just left me alone."

Kelly's stepfather told her to threaten the boys because if they "backed down," the girls would likewise stop abusing her. Kelly explained to her stepfather that she felt ill-prepared physically to threaten the boys who verbally abused her. Thus, Kelly's stepfather taught her specifically how, as Kelly put it, to "fight like a guy": "He taught me that being short made me faster, you know. He said the lower you are to the ground the faster you are. He taught me how I had that advantage, you know." Kelly and her stepfather would "play fight," and he taught her to "scrooch down when he'd swing a punch at me. And then I'd just swipe his feet out from under him or tackle him. My stepfather taught me that. And then he told me to punch them in the face." Kelly used this method of fighting in response to peer abuse by boys at school. The following is a representative example:

One day a kid [a boy] walked by me in the hall at school and called me a "wimp." He said I was just a "fucking girl," like that. Just a "girl," you know. He'd been hasslin' me like that, sayin' stuff like that, that I couldn't fight, you know. So I was tired of him, you know what I mean? So I decided to fight him right there in the hall. I wanted kids to see what I could do, you know. I ended up breaking his jaw. And I got excused for one day, and then I got to come back the next day.

I asked Kelly if this boy was physically bigger or smaller than her:

He was a little bigger but I knew I could take him. I felt I could take care of myself—I was shorter but stronger than a lot of kids. I thought about what my stepfather told me and kids kept sayin', "You're not gonna take any shit, are ya?" And so I did it to him. There were lotsa kids around, so I ran up to him and just liked tackled him, you know. I mean I real fast like got down on him and just grabbed his legs and pulled him down. He didn't even try to hit me. He just laid right there and let me pound on his face. He kinda seemed afraid to fight back, you know.

Kelly told her stepfather about the fight; he was "real proud" that she "didn't take any shit from this kid." I then asked Kelly if she was involved in other fights at school and she said: "Oh, yeah. After that anyone who called me names like 'wimp' or 'fucking girl.' They thought they were bigger and better than I was. So I proved them wrong. I'd take them down and pound on them with my fists and slam their head on the floor and tell them to shut the fuck up. And they would."

Kelly never fought girls at school, only boys. She participated in "about three dozen fights at school and I'd always win the fights with guys. Because of that I didn't need to fight girls. They saw what I could do and so they just left me alone. I was someone not to mess with, you know." Kelly's old "jock" girlfriends stopped verbally abusing her as well, and she carefully chose her battles with boys:

There are a lot of guys that are bigger than me and I wouldn't fight them, you know. Just guys kinda my size. Lotsa times I'd just beat the shit out of guys before they'd say anything. Just go up to them and smash them in the face and say, "You better keep your mouth shut," you know, like that. But the big jocks and stuff, and the preppies, the popular guys, I just left them alone 'cause they didn't want anything to do with me anyway. So it was just other guys my size that I took down. So they wouldn't try to give me shit.

Despite her assaultive violence, Kelly remained marginalized at school as "Other" by both boys and girls. Although Kelly continued to be a loner, she did gain some masculine confidence and respect at school—she "handled" each conflictual situation in a personal and individual way; she specifically targeted boys her "size" prior to any verbal abuse; and she was accorded, to a certain extent, the deference she felt she deserved. That is, through her masculine (albeit subordinate) presence at school, the boys who verbally abused her (or may do so) eventually stopped because Kelly either "took them down" or threatened to do so.

Subsequently, in eighth grade Kelly began to "hang out" on the street with the same "badass guys" that Tina "hung" with, a group of boys who represented an oppositional form of masculinity to the hegemonic masculinity of the preppy boys. The badass boys were oppositional because, according to Kelly, they frequently challenged the authority of the school (some even physically fought teachers); they regularly "skipped class" and "beat up people" at school. However, on the street they embodied hegemonic masculinity and engaged in robberies, burglaries, and group violence. Kelly joined this group because "I didn't have any friends. And they liked to do what I liked to do. And they accepted me 'cause I'm a good fighter. They were doing things like I'd seen all my life. They liked to party and get drunk, and didn't take any shit from anyone. And that was normal to me." The "badass guys" Kelly joined formed a group in which she was "the only girl who 'hung' with the guys. I was the only one that didn't dress like a girl and didn't act like a girl. All the other girls who would hang with us [the 'badass girls'] wore really tight jeans and sexy tops" (such as Tina). Kelly referred to these girls as "slutty badass girls" because "they had slept with like over a hundred guys." Kelly "hung out" with the guys (not the girls) but never engaged in sexuality with these guys because, as she put it:

> I would have sex with them if they wanted. But they don't treat me that way, you know. I'm one of them, you could say. I'd get called "ladybug" because female and male ladybugs look the same and act the same. I just got the nickname "ladybug" because I was a girl that acted like a boy. So we never talk about sex and they never come on to me and I don't come on to them.

Kelly went on to say that she was not a virgin but only had sex a few times because "sex is not that important to me." Kelly considered herself heterosexual—"I ain't no dyke"—and earlier had become sexually active around age twelve with several "jock" boyfriends who introduced her to heterosexuality. Kelly also had several "lovers" who were not in school and were considerably older than her. However, since breaking away from the "jock crowd," Kelly was now celibate and seemed comfortable with this since she otherwise was accepted by the "badass boys."

I then asked Kelly if the "slutty badass girls" fought boys like she did, and she responded: "No way, they only fight girls. And so that kinda raised my status 'cause I would fight boys, just go after boys for no reason, you know. That kinda raised my status." The slutty badass girls fought girls "mostly over shit I couldn't care about, you know. They'd give each other shit about the way they looked and then fight about it." These girls never "hassled" Kelly because "They're afraid of me, you know. They know what would happen if they did. So they didn't mess with me." Moreover, these girls rarely "hung out" with Kelly and the guys but, rather, "They'd go walking around stores and the mall. Or they'd sit down, listen to music, get high. And that was about it. They never really did anything with the guys except fuck them, you know."

Instead of going to the mall and engaging in sexuality, Kelly would play video games with the guys, wrestle with them, throw a football around with them, and occasionally she would "go out driving" and "stompin'" with them. Eventually Kelly even came to "strut" like the boys. As she pointed out: "I'd walk like them, you know. Kinda big steps with my arms hangin' down and my shoulders swaying back and forth. They liked that and I got called 'ladybug' for it." Kelly noted that her gait was quite different from the slutty badass girls because "They walked like girls, you know, with their butts tight, and short steps, standin' straight up, like that." Another embodied masculine practice Kelly participated in on the street—but the "slutty badass girls" did not—were "power barfs," which she described as follows: "Let's see. You drink beer and salt, and you'd gargle it in your mouth until it gets all foamy and then you swallow it. And then someone would hit you in the stomach and you just puke it all up. And the biggest splash and mess is the winner."

Because Kelly joined in many of the same activities practiced by the boys in the group, she "was seen as a girl, but cool like a guy": "I wasn't a guy, but I was in the guy group. Most of the time whenever the guys did something I was there and they didn't mind it, 'cause I wasn't a bitchy type of person, you know, like every single girl is. Plus I could do what they do, you know."

Although Kelly embodied a masculine presence at school and on the street, she did not "pass" as a "male." Kelly had more status in the badass group than the "slutty badass girls," yet she nevertheless was subordinate to both the preppy boys at school and the badass boys at school and on the street. As Kelly expressed her relationship with the latter boys: "The guys would always tell me what to do 'cause I'm a girl, you know. They'd say I don't know shit, and stuff like that, you know. A lot of guys are sexist and didn't want me around a lot."

Q.: How were they sexist?

A.: You know. They'd think that 'cause they're guys they are tougher and better. But I can beat the shit out of a lot of the guys. But they got to do things I didn't.

Q.: Can you give me an example?

A.: Ah, you know. Like they always got to go on robberies and burglaries, you know, and stompin', just 'cause they're guys.

Q.: You didn't always participate when the boys were involved in those crimes?

A.: No, 'cause sometimes they thought I'd get hurt, and then they'd have to deal with me. I'd get in the way and stuff like that, you know, when they gonna use knives, guns, and baseball bats.

At school Kelly navigated the structural relations among girls' groups and between badass girls and boys (for the most part she and the preppy boys ignored each other). Although initially accepted as a "jock," when Kelly enthusiastically rejected feminine bodily display by shaving the back of her head, numerous girls and boys verbally abused her and labeled her a "dyke" (by girls) and a "wimp" (by boys). The public degradation and challenge to her masculinity hurt Kelly, and initially she felt physically unable to "fight back." Predictably, Kelly discussed the situation with her stepfather. His response was to "fight back" *against boys,* and he proceeded to teach Kelly the bodily skills necessary to succeed. Kelly learned from her stepfather to manage her body in such a way to win—and she did! Thus, when Kelly's masculinity was challenged by boys her size—insightfully, she carefully avoided physical confrontations with taller and stronger boys—she would not physically "back down." And often she would target boys prior to any verbal abuse. Consequently, Kelly managed to "hold her own" in front of peers, thus embodying a masculine presence and becoming accountably masculine (albeit subordinate) at school. For this conduct Kelly received her admired stepfather's and badass boys' approval for "fighting back" against the peer abuse at school. Simultaneously, then, Kelly enjoyed a certain degree of masculine power at school and on the street—over boys and girls—yet never attained hegemonic masculine status in school or as a member of the badass group. Eventually Kelly was arrested, convicted, and placed on probation for assaultive violence ("stompin'") on the street.

PART IV

BEYOND BINARIES

• 7 •

BOYS, GIRLS, AND
EMBODIED VIOLENCE

In this chapter, I put structured action theory to work by closely examining the three major sites—the home, the school, and the street—of the boys' and girls' life histories outlined in part III. Each site contains different gender relations and different motivations for violence and nonviolence. Attention to structured gender relations, to the way in which the embodied self lives those relations, and to how such experiences motivate both violence and nonviolence in particular settings permits conceptualization of differing forms of gender construction as specific to particular milieus. Examining distinct settings captures the way individuals negotiate embodied gender practices in and through different spaces that result occasionally in assaultive violence, but also help reproduce and sometimes change structured gender relations. We begin with Lenny and Perry.

LENNY AND PERRY

Lenny and Perry are different in two important ways: Lenny was socially defined at school as a "wimp," Perry as a "bully"—thus occupying different places in the masculine hierarchy of boys at school. And Lenny was nonviolent at home, whereas Perry was violent at home. However, they were similar in that both were violent at school and on the street—but of course in different ways. In this section, I first examine their differing gender experiences at home and subsequent violence and nonviolence. Then I turn to the differing pathways to assaultive violence that Lenny and Perry embodied at school and on the street.

At Home

The life histories of Lenny and Perry show contrasting relationships between each boy and the adults in his family: Lenny experienced a nonviolent and close relationship with both biological parents; Perry suffered verbal and physical violence from his stepfather and eventual neglect from his mother, but enjoyed a warm relationship with his uncle. Consequently, different patterns of masculine attachment emerged: Lenny identified strongly with his nonviolent father; Perry was influenced by his violent stepfather and, in particular, by his benevolent (but violent) uncle. Nevertheless, both boys grew up in an environment that articulated for them a practiced definition of hegemonic masculine power. In both families the boys lived in inegalitarian gender milieus in which adult women embodied much less power than adult men. Even though both parents worked outside the home, patriarchal power seemed to be an acceptable part of familial gender relations, and this legitimized power provided the adult men with considerably greater authority in the family. Consequently, through embodied interactions in the family both boys observed hegemonic masculinity in practice by a father (Lenny) or a stepfather and uncle (Perry).

By reason of these interactions with adult males in the family, then, both boys undertook to practice what was being preached and represented—they became, in different ways, accountably masculine. It was here that both Lenny and Perry took up the fundamental project of being a masculine boy. Although constructed in different ways, each fundamental gender project is revealed in their embodiment.

Confronting the constraints and possibilities established through patriarchal gender relations at home, Lenny actively adopted certain forms of social action. Lenny's embodied practices at home articulated primarily with those of his father—his favorite things to do were activities he and "Dad" did together, such as hunting, fishing, playing catch, and playing darts. These represent the salient available practices in the home milieu that Lenny nonreflexively engaged in; thus he embodied a complicit but subordinate masculinity, as he benefited from gender privilege yet simultaneously was subordinate to his father in this setting. Lenny oriented his actions primarily for his father to acknowledge, and given that Lenny successfully engaged in such practices—Lenny's father was "real proud" of him when he shot his first deer—his masculinity was never challenged in this milieu by father or by others. Lenny was accountably masculine at home as he engaged in situationally normative intersubjective masculine conduct that helped reproduce in-home gender relations. Distancing himself from the feminine practices of his mother and sister (who performed the vast majority of domestic labor), Lenny confidently embodied a masculine presence at home and developed a close relationship with his father—he wanted to be "like Dad"— through kindred embodied interaction that seemed smooth, uneventful, socially coordinated, and nonviolent.

Perry enjoyed a warm and calm relationship with his mother after his violent and alcoholic biological father moved out. He spent considerable time outdoors, playing football and basketball with his numerous neighborhood friends. Nevertheless, Perry felt controlled and extremely bullied by his new stepfather, who otherwise ignored him. Moreover, his mother increasingly sided with the stepfather. Thus, Perry confronted new gender relations at home. And in negotiating the particular constraints and possibilities at home, he turned to and developed a warm relationship with his uncle. A significant bond matured between Perry and his uncle—the uncle was like a "real" father to Perry; he supported him emotionally, and the two spent hours playing sports, fishing, and discussing Perry's heterosexuality. Like Lenny, Perry actively adopted complicit but subordinate masculine practices principally through interaction with his uncle and, therefore, he was accountably masculine in this milieu. Perry primarily oriented his behavior in this setting toward his uncle, who he wanted to be like and by whom he wanted to be accepted.

However, as his stepfather's abuse continued unabated, Perry increasingly perceived this violence as unjust and viewed it as a masculinity challenge—he was subordinated by his stepfather and this subjection occasioned masculine ambiguity and insecurity—especially after he learned from interaction with his uncle that the "right thing to do" as "a man" was to physically "fight back." Yet it was only when Perry felt physically able to stand up to his stepfather—after his "growth spurt"—that he actually did "fight back." Perry's bodily transformation empowered him, and he subsequently responded to the masculinity challenge by reflexively engaging in assaultive violence to exhibit personal bodily power over his stepfather, thereby satisfying his uncle's criteria for "doing" hegemonic masculinity in this setting. Indeed, Perry's uncle had been in several previous physical fights with the stepfather, and as Perry put it: "I wanted to show him like my uncle did" and "It felt good to knock him down." In other words, there was a new masculine *feel* to his body as he "knocked him down": Perry now felt more accountably masculine at home by engaging in such assaultive violence—he no longer felt as subordinate and insecure. The "growth spurt" changed how Perry could now interact with and through his body, allowing him to respond to masculinity challenges as the hegemonic masculine discourse of home life suggested—that is, to physically fight back. Thus, Perry now embodied an accountably oppositional masculine presence at home, as his bodily transformation helped alter Perry's way of interacting in this milieu. Perry's bodily change allowed him to respond to his stepfather with a greater sense of masculine confidence, and such embodied practice became part of who Perry was as "a man" at home.

Like Lenny, then, for the most part Perry initially and nonreflexively developed a fundamental complicit masculine project that included such available gender practices as sports, fishing, and talking about sexuality—he became a "real boy" by engaging in situationally specific intersubjective behavior. However, Perry's fundamental gender project at home was different from Lenny's project in the sense that it entailed a reflexive commitment to assaultive violence as an accountable and embodied masculine strategy to solve interpersonal problems—he eventually challenged the hegemony of his stepfather by embodying a violent oppositional masculinity. Indeed, amongst Lenny's family members *in the home milieu*, assaultive violence was not an accountable masculine practice for solving interpersonal problems. In other words, in the two home settings there existed similar but also important different "gender practices" that were available for proper masculine embodiment: gender relations were constituted differently through the embodiment of violence or nonviolence. Thus, Lenny and Perry came to engage and embody a different *place* in in-home gender relations.

At School and on the Street

In *all* junior high schools in the United States there exists what Dan Kindlon and Michael Thompson (1999, 72–93) call the "culture of cruelty." Within school peer culture, boys face verbal abuse for any failure to conform: "Anything a boy says or does that's different can and will be used against him" (Kindlon and Thompson 1999, 73). In other words, the culture of cruelty is an interactional and intercorporeal environment that constitutes:

> a world of developing masculinity in which everything he does or thinks is judged on the basis of the strength or weakness it represents: you are either strong and worthwhile, or weak and worthless. He must also be willing to fight. Even if you have never fought, and never intend to fight, you have to pretend to yourself that you can and will. A respected boy is someone who can "handle himself." (Kindlon and Thompson 1999, 79)

Thus the culture of cruelty constructs hierarchy among boys and demands that boys respond to verbal (and physical) abuse through physical violence. Indeed, the two boys discussed in this book either participated in this culture as a bully (Perry) or as a victim (Lenny)—but both wanted to physically retaliate. The culture of cruelty at school constructs the gender practices that are available for "proper" masculine embodiment, and this culture figured significantly in each boy's narrative as a major site for masculine confrontation and embodied social action—the two boys simply took different paths to assaultive violence at school. Perry committed crimes with accomplices and in public; he was versatile in his criminality (he engaged in a variety of crimes); and when he committed violence it was exclusively assaultive violence against both acquaintances and strangers. Lenny publicly committed assaultive violence alone, against only acquaintances, and he never engaged in any other type of crime—Lenny is an assaultive specialist. What is interesting about the two life stories is not the violence per se but the differing ways violence simultaneously emerged at school, continued on the street, and was constructed in and through their respective bodies. Let us look more closely at how these differences evolved.

Research shows that the tallest and strongest boys in junior high and high school are usually the most popular—admired by peers (and parents and teachers) for their size and athletic prowess (Thorne 1993). These are the masculine "cool guys" who participate in school athletics and who—usually on weekends— defy adult authority by "partying" (e.g., experimenting with drugs, alcohol, and sex) (Eckert 1989; Foley 1990; Lefkowitz 1997). In the context of school, a boy's height and musculature increase self-esteem and prestige and create a more positive body image (Thorne 1993). Research on male adolescent development shows that boys are acutely aware of their pubertal changing selves as well as other people's responses to those changes (Petersen 1988). Boys who participate in sports, for example, state that "they take pleasure in their agency and their bodies simultaneously. They feel like they accomplish things in their bodies and in their lives" (Martin 1996, 55). That is, they "feel" masculine through bodily performance. A boy who does not have the appropriate body shape and size and who is unable to use his body in this masculine way frequently experiences distress (Petersen 1988). In the school culture of cruelty, physically small, less muscular, nonathletic boys are often labeled "wimps" and "fags" (Kindlon and Thompson 1999). In junior high and high school, masculine social hierarchies develop in relation to somatic type. Such a shared meaning of somatic differentiation affirms inequality among boys, and diverse masculinities are constructed accordingly in relation to biological development (Canaan 1987; Connell 1995; Thorne 1993). The relationship among these masculinities forms structured gender relations among boys within the social situation of the school. In short, through interaction at school, adolescent boys "make bodies matter" by constructing some bodies as more masculine than others.

As Lenny attempted to pass through the public space of the school, he came to see himself as physically "not measuring up" to the school view of the ideal masculine body. Embodied interaction at school defined Lenny differently than at home—he constituted an emasculated body, which he eventually accepted. Observing the "cool guys," Lenny perceived himself as not simply flunking the body test at school—he was not muscular or tall and could not play ball—but simultaneously as being publicly degraded for his physical size and shape. For Lenny, then, his body was a *restraint* on his in-school masculine agency—he could not do the masculine practices the "cool guys" were doing—and this somatic limitation was extremely troubling to him: he now lacked masculine self-confidence at school. Lenny's lack of bodily performance—in particular his inability to "fight back" when bullied by the "tough guys," as well as his "inferior" body shape and structure—convinced him that he was not only different from the "cool guys" at school but also was feminized in relation to them. In other words, because his body did not live up to the contextual in-school masculine expectations, this created a masculinity challenge to Lenny. Indeed, Lenny was socially constructed in school as "Other"; he embodied in-school "gender failure."

Perry, however, did physically "measure up." He participated in school sports and constructed a physical presence in school that was revered by his classmates. Perry was tall and muscular for his age. When his masculinity was challenged on the playground or in the classroom, he would not physically back down to anyone, including teachers. For Perry, his body *facilitated* masculine agency: he successfully constructed himself as a "cool guy" who was "superior" to most other boys and he embodied masculine self-confidence at school. Indeed, his ability to act out in class, bully those "inferior" to him, and physically fight when provoked convinced him of his own eminent masculine self-worth—he embodied in-school "gender success."

In short, what these two life stories reveal is that the body is an essential part of a process of negotiating self and that a boy's masculine school existence is in part dependent on the capacity for power that he embodies. As Chris Shilling (2003, 113) puts it: "This power is always an active power, a power which can be exercised on and over others. If a man's physicality is unable to convey an image of power, he is found to have little presence precisely because the social definition of men as holders of power is not reflected in his embodiment." To enjoy a sense of masculine "presence," the body must at the very least suggest the promise of forceful and vigorous physicality. In other words, the body is a crucial component of social interaction that symbolizes a boy's masculinity and therefore represents a site of either power or powerlessness.

Lenny and Perry, then, shared with others at school specific social structural space, and through their embodiment participated in the construction of common blocks of knowledge in which masculine ideals and practices were institutionalized. The particular criteria of hegemonic masculinity in their school are embedded in the social situations and in the recurrent embodied practices by which in-school gender relations are structured (Giddens 1989). Differences among boys at school hinge in part on the body—"cool guy" (Perry) is sustained through its bodily relation to situationally defined "wimp" (Lenny)—even within the same class and school context. Boys in the same social class (and even in the same working-class school) are distinguished through different constructions of the body and, therefore, masculinity. Consequently, constructs of "bully" and "wimp" inflect any class commonality with difference that produces power or powerlessness in relation to each other. One's place in gender relations among boys in school is constituted through embodied appearance and practice, resulting in differing types of assaultive violence. How specifically then did these differing types of assaultive violence unfold?

Clearly the contrasting masculinity challenges at school were important to motivating these two boys toward distinct forms of assaultive violence. As pointed out in chapter 3, masculinity challenges are contextual interactions that result in masculine degradation. Masculinity challenges—such as the peer abuse suffered by Lenny and the authoritarianism experienced by Perry—arise from interactional threats and insults from peers, teachers, parents, and from unachievable situationally defined masculine expectations. Both, in various ways, proclaim a boy subordinate in contextually defined masculine terms. Masculinity challenges arguably motivate social action toward intersubjective (because they are intercorporeal) available gender practices (e.g., "fighting back") that correct the subordinating social situation. And various forms of crime can be the result. Given that such interactions question, undermine, and/or threaten one's masculinity, only contextually "appropriate" masculine practices can help overcome the challenges.

Nevertheless, regardless of the quantity and quality of masculinity challenges, engagement in assaultive violence as an appropriate masculine response depends upon there being an opportunity for violence to occur. Social settings provide the resources and, therefore, opportunities for committing certain types of violence. Although in the cases of Lenny and Perry the motivation to commit in-school assaultive violence is activated by masculinity challenges, one must have the opportunity to engage in violence for violence to actually take place (e.g., access to a socially defined legitimate potential victim). And, as discussed below, sometimes agents actually attempt to invent a valid victim.

Indeed, Lenny's life story shows how motivation for assaultive violence is embedded in specific gender relations in distinct social settings. The three settings of home, school, and street contain different gender relations and different forms of accountability. At home, Lenny was easily accountably masculine because he effortlessly and nonreflexively engaged in the available masculine practices, and thus his masculinity was never in question in this milieu: he maintained a complicit (yet subordinate) masculine presence and self-confidence at home. However, at school Lenny faced different gender relations. Constructed as a "wimp," Lenny was disallowed participation in hegemonic masculine practices at school. He was abused often at school due to his physical size and shape, and for not demonstrating that he was "a man." Lenny accepted the in-school criterion that being hegemonically masculine meant responding to provocation with physical violence. But because he was physically small and obese relative to the bullies, Lenny was unable to respond in such a "manly" fashion. Therefore, because he did not meet the intersubjective criteria by which masculine competence is judged in school—thus exhibiting masculine uncertainty and insecurity—Lenny initially answered this masculinity challenge by becoming a loner and avoiding the "tough guys" as often as possible. Observing in-school assaults at least once a month and recognizing the somatic differences between the "tough guys," himself, and those at school assaulted by the "tough guys," Lenny became "scared to talk to kids" and after classes "ran home." In other words, the peer abuse and its meaning to Lenny developed through embodied interaction at school and it created a reflexive practice of restricted bodily movement in and out of school. School was a dangerous space for Lenny that included real overt hazards; thus, whenever possible, he intentionally chose bodily movements to avoid school and its inhabitants. Lenny's embodied practice hinged on the gestural and verbal meanings embodied in in-school others; he lacked masculine presence yet maintained a nonviolent project by avoiding school whenever possible. And through his embodied action, he inadvertently helped reproduce the masculine hierarchy among boys at school.

Nevertheless, Lenny simultaneously longed to be a "tough guy"—he wanted to be accountably masculine at school—and to be able to tell his father that he did not let others push him around. Lenny experienced verbal pressure from his father to be a "real man" at school, and thus in negotiating these situationally discursive constructs he consciously schemed and staged an attempt to "do" in-school hegemonic masculinity by verbally abusing and then assaulting a physically weaker boy in school—a "high-water"—he changed his gender strategy to engage in bullying and assaultive violence only against this particular boy. In negotiating in-school gender relations, then, Lenny now interacted with and through his body in a specific way: he prudently averted retaliating against the bullies while carefully creating a situation in which he believed masculine domination would be "successful" and would be recognized as such by others. Thus Lenny reflexively chose the hallway at school as an appropriate site for the bodily domination of an easily vulnerable boy because in this setting the violence, he hoped, would be confirmed as masculine by his peers. His attempted route out of "wimpishness" was to exhibit "fearlessness" socially by assaulting an even more subordinate "Other" than himself. However, it did not work out completely as he wished: many in the "audience" at school told him to "pick on" someone his own size. Accordingly, Lenny disconcertingly failed to alter his *place* within in-school gender relations and, thus, his masculine insecurity and emasculated presence remained unchanged.

Realizing he was unable to "do" masculinity at school—because the "highwater" was the only boy he could "beat up"—Lenny concentrated his effort at masculine recognition in his neighborhood. Because the behavioral expressions activated by the contextual masculinity challenges at school could now be directed only outside the school situation, he had to move to another milieu to become accountably masculine. In other words, Lenny's embodied interaction at school directed him toward courses of masculine social action that were realizable physically and that could be accomplished outside the boundaries of school. Lenny had a desperate need to abandon his emasculated position and fit into the hegemonic masculine model offered by the "cool guys" at school. For Lenny, then, the dominant masculine practices and thus in-school discursive criteria were not rejected. Rather, physical subordination directed him toward fixating on a specific site (his neighborhood), and on a particular form of body deployment (assaultive violence), where such practices could be realized. Moreover, Lenny had access to less-powerful people in his neighborhood and therefore to the means through which his body could attain dominant physical expression—a new masculine *feel* to his body. Given that Lenny was removed from any type of recognized and embodied masculine status in school—he was even criticized verbally for assaulting the "high-water"—interaction with the available younger and smaller boys in his neighborhood was especially attractive, and became a powerful means of doing hegemonic masculinity in the street setting.

In attempting to masculinize his body within the captivating discursive criteria of "cool guy" masculinity, then, Lenny engendered a powerful sense of self by "taking charge" on his neighborhood street and by conquering younger and smaller boys' bodies through assaultive violence. It was in the setting of the neighborhood street where Lenny's body took on a relatively new size and shape (he is physically larger and stronger than the younger boys), where it moved in a different way than at school (he was physically competent and dominant in this setting), and where it established inevitably a novel image for Lenny through the way he presented himself to the neighborhood boys and how he was read eventually by these boys. By concentrating his interactional efforts within the context of the neighborhood, Lenny was able now to transform how he interacted with and through his body—he was now hegemonically masculine in his neighborhood setting. Lenny was using his body in a new way, as force and power were now embodied in Lenny—whereas at school neither existed—and he took on a new *place* in the power hierarchy among boys and, therefore, a new embodied self in the setting of the street. The conscious choice to be violent in his neighborhood was a situational resource in which Lenny could be dominant, powerful, and masculine through bodily practice—he now embodied masculine presence. Lenny reflexively created a situation entailing new gender relations among boys in which he was in masculine control and in which he could not be criticized and rejected by an emasculating audience. In short, Lenny constructed a nonthreatening gendered context in which masculinity could be performed according to the in-school dominant criteria. Thus his fear of being seen as a "wimp" at school motivated Lenny to attempt to deny masculinity in other "Others" on the street. His embodied agency and eventual assaultive violence can be understood only as a manifestation of a strong desire to remain attached to his father—who had the shared meaning that one should only "pick the battles you can win"—and his practical accommodation to the embodied practices of the "cool guys" at school. Lenny applied the dominant in-school discursive criteria of masculinity to the neighborhood setting, and in the process created embodied masculine gender relations specific to that setting. In the brief, illusory moment of each assaultive violent incident against smaller and younger neighborhood boys who challenged his masculinity (e.g., calling him a "fag"), Lenny felt morally justified in reacting through assaultive violence. And in the process the emasculated was now the masculine—Lenny was now a "tough guy."

Lenny's assaultive violence is different from Perry's assaultive violence in an additional way—Lenny never engaged in gay bashing. This seems to be the case because Lenny's brother is gay. Lenny recognized his brother as embodying masculinity, and therefore heterosexuality was not as connected to masculinity as it was for Perry. Indeed, for Lenny sexuality is not important because, as he stated, one does not need to be sexual to be "cool." Therefore, gay bashing was conceptualized as outside the realm of masculine embodied practice, and it is obvious that such a practice would have been unacceptable to his most important masculine mentor—his father. Consequently, Lenny was defined socially as a "heterosexual wimp" who used assaultive violence exclusively against smaller and younger neighborhood boys in an attempt to nullify for himself (and his father) his emasculated status at school.

For Perry, school life was circumscribed not by verbal and physical abuse by bigger boys but, rather, by institutionalized authoritarian routine. Neither interested in nor successful at schoolwork (except during football season), Perry viewed school as irrelevant to his future and emasculating to his conception of masculinity. To Perry, school, like home, was simply another milieu in which he was tyrannized by adults. Accordingly, in negotiating in-school gender relations, Perry understood that his bodily resources empowered him reflexively to implement a physically confrontational masculinity—a masculinity that corresponded to the in-school discursive criteria of "tough-guy" masculinity. Observing the gestural and verbal meanings embodied in others at school, and being "successful" bodily at home against his stepfather, Perry joined with similar boys to carve out a specific masculine space within the school, responding in and through their bodies to its overwhelming rules and unnerving authority. Perry's embodiment permitted him physically to resist the school and in so doing to construct behavior patterns—acting out, bullying, and fighting—that set him above the "wimps" as well as above the school. Indeed, there existed an intricate interplay of Perry's body with the social process of becoming a "bully" at school. The social requirements to validate one as a masculine bully—that is, physically hurting (although not actually fighting)[1] and verbally browbeating weaker boys—is a reflexive embodied practice that connects specific actions ("smack a kid in the face" and/or "rip up his homework") with a predictable consequence to that practice ("make some kid in class look like a fool" and "everybody in the class would be laughing"). Perry consciously responded to the masculinity challenges by his friends (they "lived" to "show off" in front of each other and therefore held each other accountable to this masculine action) through consciously deploying a bodily presence in school that was revered by his classmates. Thus, through the practice of bullying to satisfy the masculinity challenge of "showing off" in front of his friends, Perry interacted with and through his body in a unique way, and in so doing he created boundaries between the bodies of "tough guys" and "wimps" within the social setting of school. Like Lenny, the body of Perry became an essential part of a process of negotiating self within the school setting and, therefore, his primary resource for masculine power, esteem, and control of space. Perry exemplified the masculine "tough guy" and "bully" who is, as Joyce Canaan (1998, 179) points out, "able to occupy space because he successfully makes his might known to others. Because he can keep the other at a distance and thereby defines the situation, he is able to operate on and control this other. He has a particular kind of male power; his presence and literal staying power imply the threat of violence."

Rather than conform to in-school formal discipline and attempt to maintain invisibility at school (as for the most part Lenny did to avoid the "tough guys"), Perry used his body in a way Lenny could not. Perry adhered to the in-school discursive criteria in which masculinity is judged by physically expressing oneself in a manner culturally idolized in the school—his public and visible sense of masculinity was constituted through his embodied practice. Perry's social action signified his membership in the "tough guy" group—he was accountably masculine—thereby securing for himself the power associated with that group. Perry expressed physical and masculine competence by exercising embodied control over in-school space; his bullying demarcated him as a "tough guy" and not as a "wimp." Perry's embodied self-confidence at the center of attention in school is the opposite of Lenny's embodied timidity at the periphery of interaction at school.

Moreover, acting out in class is also a practice that treats a teacher's insistence on right to authority as violative of his masculine "right" to embodied autonomy, independence, and control of space. In other words, being physically able to bully "wimps" in a classroom setting enacts not only masculine pleasure by "having a laugh," it likewise is seductive because it symbolically defies the authority of the teacher. To be sure, the authority embodied in the teacher was a masculinity challenge for Perry and against which he constructed in part his in-school masculinity. This is a significantly different form of embodied practice than that performed by Lenny. Conceptualizations of masculine difference, then, are dependent upon bodies and the situational discursive criteria they produce through embodied practice. Through the social action of bullying "wimps" and fighting teachers, Perry was constituted as an exemplary "tough guy," whereas his victims were embodied as emasculated inferiors. Thus, in-school masculine gender relations are reproduced through how boys interact with and through their bodies.

Eventually Perry left school, finding masculine comfort in the street group. The street group was an arena in which Perry could augment significantly his bodily expression through physical confrontation. Within the collective setting of the group, such practices as burglary and assaultive violence were particularly attractive, providing a public demonstration of bodily domination over and humiliation of others as well as embodied freedom ("the freedom to do what I wanted to do"). Assaultive violence on the street was motivated by masculinity challenges ("talking shit"), and although the group process included women, Perry constructed his "street" masculinity through sexualizing women. By consciously deploying his body in a specific way—"screwing the most girls" and "beating up faggots"—Perry additionally constituted himself in this setting as representative of dominant heterosexual in-group masculinity. Perry helped reproduce the sexual and gender relations of the street by subordinating women and gay men. Indeed, for Perry, to be accountably masculine in the street group was to engage in three major practices: "screwing" the most girls, being the "best" at fighting, and being able to "hold the most beer [and] smoke the most weed." Thus, in addition to heterosexualizing and masculinizing his body through frequent sex and gay bashing, an important criterion for hegemonic masculine embodiment was "getting hammered and fried"—having the bodily capacity to ingest large quantities of beer and marijuana.

Perry's life story shows that motivation for assaultive violence is differently embedded in specific gender relations in distinct social settings. The three sites of family, school, and street contain different gender relations, different forms of accountability, and different motivations for assaultive violence. At home, Perry's assaultive violence against his stepfather was motivated to "properly" overcome the situational masculinity challenge and insecurity and thereby be accountably masculine in the eyes of, in particular, his uncle. At school, Perry negotiated different gender relations and embodied a "tough-guy" masculinity whereby bullying "wimps" and physically attacking teachers who "get in your face" are accountably masculine. Finally, on the street, specific forms of accountability—such as frequent heterosexual sex, bashing gays, property crimes, and ingesting large quantities of illegal substances—corresponded to the particular gender relations in that milieu and, therefore, impacted his embodied masculinity.

Moreover, it is on the street where Perry exemplified the "normal criminal" of the criminological gaze—the usual violent individuals studied by criminologists. For example, Perry fit the profile reported in work on persistent property offenders (Shover 1996; Wright and Decker 1994, 1997). Perry eventually became a stalwart participant in the street culture that Richard Wright, Scott Decker, and Neal Shover emphasize in their work; he committed property crimes in part to "keep the party going." His social existence outside school consisted exclusively of "life as party" or enjoyment of "good times," with minimal emotional concern for obligations and commitments external to his immediate social setting (Shover 1996, 93)—this was now a new gender strategy, different from his embodied practices at home and at school. "Life as party" is a collective intersubjective practice that typically includes shared consumption of alcohol and other drugs through which "party pursuers" celebrate and affirm their embodied independence, thereby promoting "avoidance of routine work, freedom from being 'under someone's thumb,' and freedom to avoid or escape from restrictive routines" (Shover 1996, 95). And because such activities are cash intensive, those with the ability to sustain them over a period of time are accorded increased masculine respect and status in the street culture. As Wright and Decker (1994, 201) argue, "To be seen as hip on the street, one must be able to keep the party going." Furthermore, part of this collective party life entails occasional assaultive violence. In the street group, Perry gained masculine status, reputation, and self-respect through his continued embodied ability to "party" and by engaging in various property crimes and assaultive violence.

Conclusion

Although both Lenny and Perry were gender conformists, they simultaneously produced specific but different types of embodied masculine practices through the use of different forms of assaultive violence and nonviolence in particular settings. Both Lenny and Perry embodied situationally complicit (yet subordinate) masculinities at home, yet because Lenny did not experience masculinity challenges in this setting—as Perry did—he constructed a nonviolent masculine self, whereas Perry eventually embodied a violent masculine self in this milieu. Outside the home context different types of masculinities by Lenny and Perry emerged from practices that likewise reflected different social circumstances and different bodily resources. At school and on the street, for example, Perry embodied different configurations of masculinities, yet in each setting and though individual, these masculinities occurred within the context of different types of collective masculine projects. Lenny attempted to invalidate his subordinate masculine status in school through personal reconstruction of self in his neighborhood and not as part of a shared, collective project. Consequently, in the changing context from home, to school, and to street there existed for Lenny and Perry a transformation in the way they interacted with and through their bodies and in how assaultive violence became part of who they were as "a man." For both boys throughout the three sites, the body is a participant in generating and shaping social practice. Moreover, examining different settings allows us to conceptualize the way in which the embodied self negotiates gender relations differently, depending upon one's occupancy of a particular *place* in situational gender relations and the embodied practices through which boys engage that place.

Although different in these crucial ways, Lenny and Perry are similar in that their differing forms of assaultive violence in different settings rely on bodily deployment and performance. Each boy, in his individually telling way, exercised embodied power over other bodies. Perry subordinated and oppressed "wimps" and teachers ("to show off") and gay males (for "talking shit") through bullying and assaultive violence. Lenny subordinated and oppressed younger and smaller boys (for verbally abusing him and challenging him to a fight) through assaultive violence. Both boys experienced their everyday situationally specific worlds from particular bodily positions, and their bodies, in turn, entered negotiated social interactions and shaped future social practices. For Lenny and Perry, then, their sense of masculinity was fashioned by, in particular, their bodily relations at home, in school, and on the street; and their bodies—as resources for social action—restrained or facilitated possible masculine agency and subsequent practice. The embodied masculine self of Lenny and Perry resulted, then, from their interaction with and through their body in particular social settings. And although there existed unity and coherence in their fundamental gender projects across sites, the actual accomplishment of that project varied situationally, and often was occasioned by gendered contradictions and ambiguities. In short, for both Lenny and Perry, the mind–body and sex–gender binaries were thoroughly interfused—their specific masculinities were lived in and through their bodies, yet were constituted differently depending upon the particular situational gender relations in distinct settings.

Let us now turn our attention to Tina and Kelly.

TINA AND KELLY

Important differences in Tina's and Kelly's life stories were that Tina engaged in assaultive violence at home whereas Kelly did not, and Tina was not violent on the street but Kelly was; yet they were similar in that they both committed assaultive violence at school. Nevertheless, "doing gender" does not always mean living up to—or attempting to live up to—situationally normative conceptions of gender (as both Lenny and Perry did); rather, "It is to engage in action *at the risk of* being held accountable for it" (Fenstermaker and West 2002, 30). This social condition permits innovation and flexibility in gender construction, and the ongoing potentiality for normative transgression, which for Tina and Kelly occurred in varying ways at home, at school, and on the street. In other words, one of the major gender differences between Lenny and Perry and Tina and Kelly is that the boys' assaultive violence was normatively conformist, whereas the girls' assaultive violence was normatively transgressive. Let us examine more closely Tina's and Kelly's life experiences in the different settings of home, school, and street.

At Home

Tina perceived family gender relations as unjust and injurious, specifically concerning her mother, who daily faced physically violent subjugation. Although

Tina and her mother mutually supported and protected each other, until Tina grew larger physically (in height) she could do nothing substantial about the harsh brutality endured by her mother. Prior to her somatic change, Tina experienced gender insecurity and was "forced" to invest in verbal protection of her mother and, therefore, remained solely accountably feminine: alternatives simply were not feasible, as her body was a *restraint* on her agency. However, with bodily changes, Tina was able to engage in physical protection, a gender normative transgressive and contradictory practice that changed the overall gender relations at home. In both cases, Tina drew on the gestural and verbal meanings constructed by and through the bodies of her mother and stepfather. The stepfather's abuse of her mother (and Tina) represented a hegemonic masculine embodied practice in this particular setting because the specific patriarchal gender relations at home connected violence to the stepfather's hegemonic masculinity and nonviolence to the mother's emphasized femininity. For the stepfather, then, his battering was a predatory practice that attempted to stabilize a structure of masculine dominance and control in gender relations at home. Tina came to conceptualize the situationally emphasized feminine response to the battering as lacking substance and adopted from her stepfather assaultive violence as the only meaningful behavior to protect her mother—her body now *facilitated* masculine agency; there existed a new *feel* to her body. Although Tina reflexively utilized a situationally specific gendered masculine practice to defend her mother—she hit him in the face with her fists "just like he did to Mom"—Tina's assaultive violence had a different meaning to her than the battering had to the stepfather. For Tina, engaging in assaultive violence at home constructed a new discourse in this setting: a protective practice that destabilized masculine dominance and control. Consequently, Tina's assaultive violence against her stepfather was simultaneously normatively transgressive and accountably feminine, thereby constructing an oppositional femininity by *redefining gender difference* at home. Tina now embodied a different type of self, entailing a more self-confident way of acting in this setting. Able to physically "fight back" against her stepfather, Tina now interacted with and through her body in a new way.

In grappling then with the constraints and possibilities set by patriarchal gender relations at home, beginning at age twelve Tina nonreflexively engaged predominantly in emphasized feminine behavior—she constructed a fundamental feminine project—but occasionally she reflexively appropriated physically violent practices (situationally defined as masculine) designed to protect her mother (and ultimately herself) from patriarchal oppression. Realizing the ineffectiveness of strictly and accountably emphasized feminine practices, Tina appropriated from her stepfather what seemed to be the only accessible embodied alternative—assaultive violence—that actually solved the problem; the stepfather moved out and the in-home gender relations were reconfigured in a more egalitarian way.

Similar to Perry, then, what this scenario highlights is the social, interactive, and embodied nature within which Tina's assaultive violence at home was constructed. Tina negotiated particular in-home gender relations by embracing and resisting certain intersubjective gender practices of copresent interactants—her parents—in this specific milieu. The relationships of those involved in these interactions and their embodied practices impacted the conscious choice Tina made to act in a distinct way, and the particular gender relations in this setting influenced the situationally specific reflexive motivation for her assaultive violence—protection. Thus, Tina's assaultive violence at home embodied a situationally defined masculine practice (assaultive violence) that simultaneously manifested an accountably emphasized feminine motive (protection of mother). By "fighting back" against her stepfather, then, Tina entered the realm of gendered power that had heretofore been the province of her stepfather—she momentarily occupied a new *place* in in-home gender relations—while simultaneously preserving her important and complementary relationship with mother. Consequently, at home Tina redefined what it meant to be *a girl*. Although Tina's assaultive violence was based in part on an intentional rejection of her mother's "feminine" response to patriarchal violence, Tina's choice to physically protect her mother was significantly different from Perry's assaultive violence against his stepfather in the sense that it was *not* performed specifically to accomplish masculinity. Perry's assaultive violence against his stepfather was intended to prove his masculinity to himself, his stepfather, and his uncle. Tina's assaultive violence was an unintended masculine practice (albeit intended as protection), yet constructed by adherence to a masculine discursive criterion set by her stepfather's embodied action. Consequently, by occasionally engaging in such masculine social action Tina redefined what it meant to be a girl in this setting.

Nevertheless, after the stepfather moved out and was no longer part of the family interaction, Tina eschewed assaultive violence and once again became solely nonviolent—and exclusively constructed an emphasized feminine self—at home. Thus, Tina's in-home assaultive violence was a momentary and provisional gender normative transgression and contradiction—an oppositional femininity challenging the stepfather's hegemony—embedded in specific patriarchal gender relations at a particular time.

Kelly of course was different from Tina in that she actively rejected nearly all aspects of femininity; she did so not to challenge patriarchal oppression but because "doing" femininity was painfully confining and required unexciting domestic labor. Accordingly, Kelly distanced herself from in-home emphasized feminine discursive criteria (as represented by her sisters and mother), even to the extent of discounting her mother as a mentor: for Kelly, she was an intoxicated and weak person living a lackluster life. There were clear advantages, from Kelly's point of view, for eschewing femininity and practicing masculinity. The latter permitted Kelly to enjoy tranquil (rather than tumultuous) interaction with her stepfather. Moreover, it sanctioned practices she conceptualized as "fun"; for example, public "burping" and "farting." For Kelly, then, doing femininity restricted bodily mobility and freedom; doing masculinity offered a semblance of autonomous self-rule in the home when compared to the status of her sisters and mother. Kelly's interaction at home and alliance with her stepfather clearly was fraught with tension and fear—she allied with her stepfather to, in part, avoid succumbing to his violence, and to avoid being rendered "weak" like her mother. Kelly enjoyed more privileges than her mother and sisters, yet remained subordinate to, and under the domination of, her stepfather.

By intimately attaching herself to her stepfather, then, Kelly reflexively opened the possibility to become accountably "Daddy's boy" and to reap the gendered benefits such embodied social action promised. Arguably, Kelly drew on the practices and subsequent discursive criteria at home, and—like Lenny and Perry—constructed a complicit (albeit subordinate) masculinity in this setting by benefiting from the oppression of her sisters and her mother. Kelly was accountable to—and wholly endorsed—her stepfather's in-home hegemonic masculine project. Yet she did not embody hegemonic masculinity at home. Rather, Kelly reflexively constructed a masculinity that included partial procurement of the in-home "patriarchal dividend" without doing the violence of its chief practitioner. Although Kelly gained from the subordination of her sisters and mother, she was not a "frontline trooper" (Connell 1995, 79). In other words, Kelly subverted emphasized femininity while simultaneously perpetuating oppressive and dichotomous gender relations at home—her body *facilitated* masculine agency in this setting—and therefore occupied a specific masculine presence and place in in-home gender relations.

From a young age, then, Kelly attempted in all aspects of home life to be accountably masculine—this was her fundamental gender project and was revealed in her embodiment. Kelly's stepfather held her accountable to masculine embodiment, and she did not resist—even though, to some extent, her mother attempted to hold her accountable to emphasized femininity. At home Kelly experienced two competing configurations of accountability—and therefore gender ambiguity—yet reflexively chose to reject femininity and embrace masculinity. Thus, Kelly embodied masculinity by engaging in situationally normative complicit masculine conduct at home (e.g., "throwing" her plate to the side after finishing a meal in front of the TV), even to the extent of supporting her stepfather's violence (but not engaging in such violence herself). Kelly endorsed physical violence as a legitimate response to interpersonal conflict—being "hassled"—and she seemingly admired her stepfather for practicing violence against her mother. Troubled by the negative relationship with her mother, Kelly had no interest in attempting to protect her mother from her stepfather's violence. Consequently, rather than contributing to social change in gender relations at home as did Tina, Kelly's behavior helped validate in-home patriarchal relations by constructing practices that the home milieu recognized as gendered masculine. Accordingly, Kelly endorsed and defied certain practices of co-present interactants—her parents and sisters—in the specific milieu of home. The particular situational interaction at home resulted in Kelly becoming accountably masculine in this milieu, yet simultaneously practicing embodied nonviolence. Like Lenny, then, Kelly's experiences at home highlight the time- and place-specific aspects of doing gender through embodied nonviolence. Kelly had no need to engage in violence at home because she constructed a complicit masculine self in part sustained through the violence of her stepfather. Consequently, as a girl embodying a masculine self, Kelly interacted with and through her body in a specific way by *blurring gender difference* at home—she embodied gender nonconformity.

At School and on the Street

Although primary and secondary schools contain a variety of gender relations among, for example, teachers, administrators, and students, during the interviews of Tina and Kelly I concentrated on the gender relations among preppy girls, badass girls, and badass boys in their school. These relations are underpinned by a structure of inequality in which the badass girls are subordinated to both the badass boys and the preppy girls. The interview data show that such unequal relations are important particularly for understanding certain aspects of both Tina's and Kelly's in-school assaultive violence and, eventually, violence or nonviolence on the street.

Finding social support in the badass group after being rejected by the popular preppies, at age twelve Tina became accountably "bad" by in part embodying an exaggerated femininity; that is, a badass girl was accountably feminine at Tina's and Kelly's school if she looked good through thinness, wore the appropriate provocative clothing, hairstyle, and considerable makeup, and was heterosexually active, ideally with a boyfriend. Thus, we can see the intersubjective and intercorporeal nature of Tina's new feminine embodiment and how she now interacted with and through her body differently than when she was a "preppy."

To be sure, additional aspects of being accountable in the badass girls' group required a specific "Don't-mess-with-me" and "crazy" bodily comportment, and engagement in a situationally defined masculine practice (assaultive violence) under specific in-school circumstances and forms of interaction. Although both boys and girls were similar in the sense of engaging in assaultive violence at school when their gendered self was under threat, Tina exclusively committed in-school assaultive violence when she was subjected to a femininity challenge by a preppy girl. Femininity challenges (like masculinity challenges) are contextual interactions that result in feminine degradation. Femininity challenges arise from interactional threats and insults from peers, teachers, parents, and from situationally defined feminine expectations that are not achievable. For example, when the preppy girls would remark to Tina that she looked "like a whore," or called her a "slut," or a "tomboy," they were publicly deviantizing Tina's femininity—these were preppy girl attempts to hold Tina accountable to emphasized femininity for her nonconformity. Assaultive violence invalidates the preppy girl edicts and proclaims Tina's allegiance to the badass girls—she was accountably *bad* because her body *facilitated* such social action; once again, there was a specific new *feel* to Tina's body in terms of what it could do. In other words, the presence of the badass girls and their support for such bodily action legitimated Tina's embodied response to the preppy challenge. Thus, like at home, Tina negotiated particular in-school gender relations by embracing and resisting certain practices of copresent interactants—in particular, badass and preppy girls. The relationship among those involved in these interactions impacted the choices she made, and the particular gender relations among girls influenced her in-school motivation for assaultive violence—nullifying a negative and insecure feminine representation. Tina fought preppy girls at school to defend her badass image as a girl and, therefore, her assaultive violence was a form of resistance against preppy girl attempts at social control. Fighting preppy girls was an available gender practice that demonstrated a sense of power in a gendered environment that provided badass girls—like Tina—with little power. And by taking up a practice that is considered masculine at school—assaultive violence in which she "fight[s] like guys"—Tina constructed her feminine self in opposition to emphasized femininity and thereby *redefined gender difference* in this setting. In the school setting, Tina practiced gender reflexivity because she carefully considered the content and the effects of her assaultive social action as *a girl*—it was the only meaningful action that simultaneously (according to the badass discursive criteria) and legitimately "got back" at the preppy girls.

Moreover, Tina's life story alerts us to the fact that motivations for assaultive violence by girls—like boys—are embedded in specific gender relations in distinct social settings. The three settings of home, school, and street contain different gender relations, different forms of accountability, and different motivations for assaultive violence. At home, Tina's assaultive violence against her stepfather was a form of normative gender transgression (that was gendered masculine) with the goal of protecting her mother against patriarchal violence. At school Tina negotiated different gender relations and found herself confronted by two stalwart, yet distinct and competing, configurations of accountability. The preppy girls' exclusion of Tina from their group and their involvement in forms of verbal peer abuse were situationally emphasized feminine practices specific to that group by which they attempted to hold Tina accountable to in-school emphasized femininity. Tina eventually rejected that group's form of femininity and subsequently was held accountable to "bad-girl femininity." Indeed, it was these distinct constructions of femininity that defined each group. Consider, for example, the particular in-group meaning of violence; for the preppy girls, only verbal peer abuse was accountable (interpersonal violence was masculine and therefore inappropriate for girls); for the badass girls, interpersonal violence was accountable under specific circumstances, such as a femininity challenge or an abusive boyfriend (verbal violence was "catty" and unacceptable for girls). Accordingly, girls' groups in the same social setting construct specific configurations of accountability and particular meanings of gender difference based on violence. Finally, on the street Tina experienced different gender relations involving subordination to the badass boys (that disallowed her participation in "stompin'") and no interaction with preppy girls. Consequently, and although she maintained a tough bodily comportment in feminine attire—and thus a specific type of feminine self—Tina simply "partied" on the street and was therefore nonviolent in this setting; she embodied a particular *place* in the specific street gender relations (that differed from school) and therefore constructed a situationally specific form of emphasized femininity in this setting.

Kelly's negotiation of the same in-school gender relations among girls differed from Tina's, as she initially positioned herself as a "jock." Yet because of her masculine appearance and practice—especially shaving the back of her head—she was ostracized and labeled a "dyke" (by girls) and a "wimp" (by boys). Although Kelly wanted to challenge these attempts to "make" her accountably feminine by responding in a situationally masculine way (assaultive violence) her body initially *restrained* her agency. For Kelly, her body did not live up to the contextual in-school masculine expectations—physically fighting back when verbally abused—and, consequently, it created an in-school masculinity challenge. Unlike Tina who was solely verbally abused by "preppy girls," Kelly was socially constructed as "Other" by both boys and girls—she was neither accountably feminine nor accountably masculine. Indeed, Kelly and Lenny were similar in the sense that both were subjected to homophobic verbal abuse.

Determined, Kelly turned to her stepfather for help in overcoming her masculine insecurity: he taught her how to manage her body in an accountably masculine fashion. Kelly's body became the object of her social action as she worked on it in an attempt to transform her body into an "appropriate" masculine force for the particular school setting. Although prudently avoiding boys physically larger than her—the vast majority of whom ignored Kelly anyway—she intentionally created situations where physical domination of boys would be seen by others as admirable. Her physical sense of masculinity was derived in part, then, from her ability to change her body through social practice into a "proper" fighting machine—she constructed a more confident sense of self, a new way of interacting with and through her body in the school setting. Indeed, Kelly specifically concentrated on beating up boys (similar in physical size) who verbally abused her at school, and choosing spaces (e.g., the hallway) where her assaultive violence would be confirmed as masculine by her peers. She developed not only a "Don't-mess-with-me" reputation—a reputation significantly different from Tina in that it was directed at boys and girls—but also satisfied her father's criteria for doing appropriate masculine violence.

Differing from Lenny, Kelly actually became accountably masculine at school—she embodied masculine presence in this setting—because her gender reflexive conduct secured competence for her to engage in violence when confronted with a masculinity challenge. Kelly's motive for fighting at school—to exhibit embodied power over boys—was similar to Perry's and Lenny's (but different from Tina's) motives; they also experienced masculinity challenges at school, although each in different ways. By exercising bodily power on and over certain boys, Kelly established a sense of embodied masculine presence at school, albeit a subordinate masculinity, and thus a new masculine *feel* to her body. To engage in such acts was to be accountably masculine at school because the particular gender relations in that setting gave meaning to this type of violence as gendered masculine. Thus, the Lenny–Kelly juxtaposition demonstrates a somewhat unique and contradictory situation where a girl (Kelly) embodies masculinity while a boy (Lenny) does not in the particular social setting of the school.

Like Tina, Kelly eventually engaged in what Barrie Thorne (1993, 121–134) labels "gender crossing," or when individuals successfully join in the groups of the other gender. However, Kelly occupied a different *place* in gender relations on the street than Tina and, thereby, became a practicing member of the badass boy group rather than the badass girl group. In such a situation the social meaning of gender difference is muted and "gender tokens participate on the terms of the majority and not as 'the other sex.'" Gender crossing can be accomplished only, Thorne argues, "if gender-marking is minimized and heterosexual meanings are avoided" (1993, 132).

This is exactly what happened when Kelly joined the badass boy group on the street. Kelly did not position herself as a "slutty badass girl" but, rather, attempted to become "one of the guys" (Miller 2001). Kelly's embodied appearance and practices—such as engaging in assaultive violence against boys, "power barfs," and performing the appropriate "strut"—minimized gender difference, and heterosexual meanings were irrelevant during her interaction in this group. Moreover, Kelly occasionally would participate—alongside the boys—in "stompin'," or group assaultive violence, against other groups of boys. Thus, Kelly's embodied violence on the street was very different from Tina's embodied nonviolence in this milieu because the latter was accountably feminine whereas the former was part of an overall masculine cultural context that clearly gendered such behavior as masculine in the badass group setting. Nevertheless, systematic gender inequalities ensured that Kelly's experience as a masculine badass-group member could never be the same as the boys'. Thus, Kelly constructed different masculinities in different settings, yet her embodied practices in all three milieus did not *erase* gender differences, but rather, simply *blurred* them.

As the case study of Kelly demonstrates, the materiality of bodies matters—masculine embodiment by girls is sometimes enacted and practiced. Kelly learned from her stepfather how to manage her body in a particular way—physical retaliation—and thus her body was transformed from *constraining* to *facilitating* masculine agency at school and eventually on the street. Altering her embodied practices to "fight back" successfully increased Kelly's masculine self-confidence and metamorphosed the way in which she interacted with and through her body at school and on the street. Engaging in assaultive violence effectively enhanced both her masculine power and sense of agency. In negotiating her embodiment through interaction with her stepfather, then, Kelly employed new bodily skills at school and on the street to become largely—although not completely—accountably masculine in both milieus. Kelly constructed a new gendered self, and in the process helped form new masculine relations at school and on the street.

Accordingly, Kelly's life story, like Tina's, helps us understand the relationship between embodied violence or nonviolence and masculinities by girls in differing milieus. Indeed, Kelly became masculine through routinized embodied practices—she experienced her embodied self as masculine in everyday life at home, at school, and on the street. Thus, Kelly's embodiment was at once a site of gender resistance—from her surface covering (e.g., clothing) and body alteration (e.g., shaved back of head) to her particular practices (e.g., public burping and farting, power barfs, strut, and assaultive violence)—yet simultaneously it reproduced gender inequality in all three settings.

Conclusion

Although more research clearly is necessary, Tina's and Kelly's life stories alert us to the fact that motivation for assaultive violence *and* nonviolence by girls is embedded in specific gender relations in distinct social settings. The life history data highlight the time- and place-specific aspects of Tina and Kelly doing gender through assaultive violence and nonviolence, depending upon the particular gender relations and their position in those relations. Indeed, such gender relations specific to certain settings resulted in both girls embodying nonviolence in different contexts—Kelly at home and Tina on the street—as well as assaultive violence in the same (the school) and different (the home vs. the street) milieus. In addition, both girls embodied power and powerlessness in specific settings. Regarding the former, Tina came to embody power over her stepfather and over some girls at school and Kelly embodied power over certain boys at school and over the "slutty badass girls" in the badass group. Thus, examining such distinct settings as the home, the school, and the street captures the way in which co-present interactants negotiate situationally specific intersubjective embodied gender practices that reproduce and sometimes change structured gender relations. For both girls, their specific gender constructions (such as fundamental masculine or feminine gender projects) were based on interaction with and through their bodies, yet were constituted differently depending upon the particular situational gender relations in distinct settings. In all three settings, the bodies of Tina and Kelly were participants in generating and shaping social practice. And although there existed unity and coherence to their gender projects across sites, the actual accomplishment of that project varied situationally, and often occasioned by gendered contradictions and ambiguities. Thus, as with Lenny and Perry, for both Tina and Kelly the mind–body and sex–gender binaries were interfused throughout their life histories.

Tina and Kelly, then, shared numerous similarities with Lenny and Perry, such as engaging in both masculine practices and assaultive violence, as well as encountering gender challenges, albeit in different ways. Indeed, for all four teenagers, significant motivating factors for engagement in assaultive violence were found in particular masculinity and femininity challenges. Nevertheless, Tina and Kelly also experienced certain social conditions that Lenny and Perry did not. This chapter ends with two brief discussions of these differences.

First, both Tina and Kelly grew up in patriarchal families in which masculine violence was an integral part. Although Perry also grew up in such a family, Lenny did not. This difference is not surprising given the conclusions of previous research comparing violent boys and girls—violent girls disproportionately live in a world in which they are the victims of, or they frequently witness other girls' and women's victimization of, male violence (Chesney-Lind and Pasko 2004; Schaffner 2004). Nevertheless, what the life stories of Tina and Kelly further highlight is not simply the violence in their lives—and the fear of possible victimization at home—but the differing ways girls respond to such violence and how they embody agency on behalf of themselves and/or others. Interacting with and through their bodies within the constraints of violent patriarchal relations, Tina and Kelly resisted such violence in individually telling ways, embodying masculine practices for self-protection (Kelly) or for self-protection and the protection of a loved one (Tina).

Second, although all four youth were encouraged in different ways by adults to "fight back" physically against abusive peers at school—and Lenny, Perry, and Kelly were all closely attached (albeit in different ways) to an adult male (a father, an uncle, and a stepfather, respectively)—a major difference between the boys and the girls existed regarding their relationship with their mothers (although this later changed for Perry). Both Lenny and Perry had close and respectful relationships with their mothers; Tina and Kelly viewed their mothers as "weak" individuals who were powerless in interaction with their stepfathers. This finding likewise is consistent with previous research, which discloses that violent girls are much less attached to their mothers than are nonviolent girls and boys and violent boys (Artz 2004). This also may have implications for why, in part, both Tina and Kelly became hostile and aggressive toward other girls. For example, in Schaffner's (2004) recent study of violent girls in California, she found such girls often witnessed their mothers and other women being degraded and subordinated by men; consequently, the violent girls came to view women and girls as worthy of less respect in an attempt to "fit in" to specific gender relations that devalue women and girls.

In sum, then, the life histories and analyses I have presented reveal both similarities and differences between assaultive boys and girls and the fallacy of the mind–body, sex–gender, and gender difference binaries. In particular, criminologists no longer can ignore similarity and difference or reject the body as domain for theoretical and empirical enquiry. Use of the above binaries removed any connection among the body, gender, and crime as well as how boys and girls and men and women may occasionally embody gender similarity in crime and violence. These four life stories demonstrate that the body is not a passive and neutral *thing* but, rather, it is a material and necessary component of violent and nonviolent gendered social action by both boys and girls. Indeed, through embodied social action in particular settings, individuals occasionally do gender similarity and gender difference through assaultive violence and nonviolence.

Moreover, these life stories show that gender difference may be disrupted through embodied social action. It is to this topic that we turn in chapter 8.

• 8 •

DISRUPTING
DIFFERENCE

The life histories of Lenny, Perry, Tina, and Kelly show in at least two distinct ways that gender difference may be disrupted through embodied social action. First, the case studies reveal that gender difference is not simply constructed between boys and girls (as most criminologists contend), but it is also prominent among boys and among girls as well as individually *across* the three settings. To be sure, by examining distinct settings we can capture the way boys and girls negotiate embodied gender practices differently in and through specific spaces that result in assaultive violence and nonviolence and that help reproduce and sometimes change structured gender relations. In other words, boys and girls embody gender difference differently depending upon the specific setting in which it occurs. Second, the study demonstrates that "sex" is not a "natural" foundation of gender. In particular, the cases of Tina and Kelly show that they both in different ways eschewed feminine, and enthusiastically undertook masculine, practices. Thus, Tina's and Kelly's life stories challenge the validity of a binary conception of gender and crime in that the two girls engaged not only in similar practices as boys (assaultive violence), but in so doing they simultaneously embodied gender differently from emphasized femininity— gender does not simplistically "follow in the footsteps" of "sex." Consequently, these case studies point to the importance of examining how certain contexts and situations result in gender similarity between boys and girls and how girls may occasionally construct masculine practices (Tina) or a fundamental masculine gender project (Kelly).

Nevertheless, the life histories of Tina and Kelly require further reflection because as these two girls acted in ways similar to boys—by engaging in assaultive violence—they did not entirely escape gender difference. Indeed, the life stories of Tina and Kelly undeniably push our thinking in more sophisticated and complex directions. Not only do these girls' life stories exhibit the weaknesses of "difference theories" based on the mind–body and sex–gender binaries, they also problematize any tendency to assume an undifferentiated sameness across genders. In this final chapter, then, I extend the analysis of Tina and Kelly by examining more closely their particular relationship to masculine practices and how their life stories actually disrupt gender difference while simultaneously reproducing it.

UNDIFFERENTIATED SAMENESS

In the 1970s, Freda Adler (1975, 15) assumed an undifferentiated sameness across genders by arguing that because of the second wave of the women's movement, adolescent girls were becoming more masculine, resulting in an increasing number of them using "weapons and wits to establish themselves as full human beings, capable of violence and aggression as any man." For Adler (1977, 101), because of "liberation," the "'second sex' had risen" by the mid-1970s and, therefore, adolescent girls became increasingly aggressive, violent, and masculine; that is, gender sameness (rather than difference) was now the order of the day. However, the idea that alleged "liberation" results in increasing masculinity and, thus, violence on the part of adolescent girls (and women generally) was quickly and soundly criticized (Belknap 2001, 54). Moreover, such a view defines, for example, girls like Tina and Kelly as simply no longer authentically *girls*. Indeed, in 1995, I published a paper arguing that criminology did not at that time possess the theoretical language capable of representing violence by adolescent girls because criminologists like Adler simplistically perceived girls' (and women's) violence from the perspective of violent acts by boys and men (Messerschmidt 1995). As Margaret Shaw (1995, 122) also pointed out in the mid-1990s, the criminological image of violence by women "is based on that of male violence—macho, tough, aggressive; we have no ways of conceptualizing violence by women except in terms of its 'unnaturalness.'" Indeed, in a society that formally recognizes only two genders (because allegedly there exists only two sexes), it follows that if an individual is not one (feminine), then she must be the other (masculine). In such a conceptualization the only variation possible is an exchange of one gender for its "opposite"; there are no conceivable alternatives to the dichotomy of "male" and "female." Consequently, we should not be surprised of Adler's formulation, and in response, after reviewing the secondary ethnographic literature on "girls in the gang," I suggested in my 1995 paper that criminology required theory that is sensitive to how women and girls *as women and girls* occasionally commit violence. And in doing so, that ethnographic literature lead me to introduce the concept of bad-girl femininity.

BAD-GIRL FEMININITY

Much research on gender and crime has neglected the fluidity of embodied gender practices, especially among girls. I attempted to overcome this neglect in my 1995 paper on gang girls, arguing that in "the daily life of the youth gang, girls not only participate in the social construction of [gender] difference but also engage in practices common to boys" (Messerschmidt 1995, 178). The paper demonstrated how structured action theory maintains a dynamic approach to gender through its ability to examine the diverse ways in which gang girls actively embody gender in different situations of the gang setting. Indeed, the first half of the paper concentrated on various ways gender difference is embodied, whereas the emphasis of a relatively long and final section focused on commonalities across gender. The ethnographic studies I relied upon indicated that gang girls not only valued traditional notions of femininity, they also united with boys physically to defend the "hood." I noted that gang girls are distinguished from nongang girls through their acceptance and participation in gang fighting, and that fighting by both boys and girls establishes loyalty to the "hood" and to the group. Furthermore, I pointed out that because "gender is not static but dynamic, in a race- and class-specific context where 'hood' is elevated to preeminence (that is, neighborhood differences become highly salient) the path for similarity in behavior is much less obstructed" (Messerschmidt 1995, 182). My conclusion was that gang girls embody a combination of gender difference practices (such as child care) and gender similar practices (such as violence to defend the "hood")—each practice justified by appropriate circumstances (Messerschmidt 1995, 184). The case of gang girls exhibits a unique fluidity of gender in which certain gender practices are emphasized or avoided depending on the social setting. In addition, I compared this conclusion to Barrie Thorne's work on boys and girls in elementary schools:

> Barrie Thorne (1993) recently reported in her important work on gender in elementary schools that when classroom events are organized around an absorbing task, such as a group art project, the cooperation encouraged between boys and girls helps to clear a path toward gender similarity. Likewise, for both boys and

girls in the gang, one of the most absorbing tasks is common defense of the "hood." Indeed, the symbolic essence of the gang is triggered and becomes meaningful only through interneighborhood conflict. In this social situation, gang boys and girls unite and work together to protect "their neighborhood" from the threat of adjacent neighborhood gangs. . . . Under such conditions gender difference becomes secondary to group difference and the result is a social site for the construction of "bad-girl" femininity. (Messerschmidt 1995, 184)

In other words, occasionally gang girls engage in behavior (physical violence) that is similar to behavior usually associated with boys and men. I argued that this fluctuating gender embodiment from difference to similarity and back to difference takes place for two reasons. First, in the social situation of interneighborhood conflict, gang boys and girls unite on the basis of "hood"—and, therefore, group differences become more salient than gender differences—which clears the path for more similarity in gender behavior. And second, in other aspects of gang life gang girls are assessed successfully as girls, even when actively participating in street violence.[1] The concept "bad-girl femininity" was developed specifically to capture the salience and fluidity of gender embodiment by gang girls. Much of the ethnographic research I relied upon noted that girls who were "down with the gang"—that is, they successfully demonstrated bodily strength and toughness—referred to themselves in a similar way as Tina and Kelly: they dubbed themselves *bad girls*.[2] The evidence before me then suggested that gang girls maintained a clear sense of themselves as girls. For example, one of the sources I relied upon was Ann Campbell's (1993, 133) important work on "girls in the gang," which argued that gang-girl concern, "with . . . appearance, their pride in their ability to attract men, [and] their sense of responsibility as mothers left me in no doubt that they enjoyed being women. They didn't want to be like men and, indeed, would have been outraged at such a suggestion" (1993, 133).

Thus, the concept "bad-girl femininity" attempted to symbolize this situational involvement by gang girls both in behavior similar to boys—that is, "acting bad" through violent practices—and in behavior different from boys, *without changing their fundamental gender project*. Indeed, my conclusion supported Thorne's (1993, 121) notion of "gender crossing" as "the process through which a girl or a boy may seek access to groups and activities of the other gender." Thorne specifically rejected the word "passing" because in the "crossing" situations she observed, the "boys and girls did *not* pretend to be of the other gender." Thus, for Thorne—which is similar to the argument in my 1995 paper—the girls in her study who "crossed" did not change their fundamental feminine gender project, did not adorn themselves in masculine attire, yet would occasionally engage—like Tina—in what were defined situationally as masculine practices.

I concluded therefore that in the specific social situation of street gangs, such gender fluidity is normative behavior for girls (but it does challenge emphasized femininity in the broader culture and differs from the femininity constructed by nongang girls). In the gang milieu, activities appropriate to girls' gender construction involve bodily strength and power as resources for publicly demonstrating individual proficiency at defending the "hood" by conquering adversary gang girls. I argued that what is usually considered atypical behavior by girls outside the social situation of the gang is, in fact, normalized within the social context of interneighborhood conflict; gang-girl violence in this situation is encouraged, permitted, and privileged by both boys and girls. In other words, within the context of many street gangs, girls' involvement in fighting rival gang girls is "specifically unremarkable and thus not worthy of more than a passing remark, because they are seen to be in accord with culturally [that is, gang] approved standards" (West and Zimmerman 1987, 136).

Given that gang girls realize their behavior is accountable to other girls and boys in the gang, they construct their embodied actions in relation to how those actions will be interpreted by others in the same social context. These girls, I argued, are embodying gender in terms of activities appropriate to the specific social situation of the gang. Even though gang girls *situationally* engage in similar behavior as gang boys (physically violent practices), this does not call into question their "femaleness." Indeed, the evidence I worked with indicated that gang girls are emphatic about their femininity. For example, I pointed out that gang girls "are 'very fussy' over gender display (clothes, hair, makeup)" and, thus, "for the most part display themselves as feminine in culturally 'appropriate' ways" (Messerschmidt 1995, 183–184). The research then indicated that gang girls' practices of bodily empowerment, such as engaging in physical violence, often occur contemporaneously with conspicuous displays and practices of femininity. Consequently, my conclusion was that the majority of—but clearly not all—gang girls constructed a situationally specific "bad-girl femininity" that dramatized the seemingly incongruent relationship between traditional feminine appearance and practices and public bodily empowerment. Gang girls were negotiating how to fit into the unequal gendered structural arrangements of the gang by making use of available gender practices and other resources at hand. Indeed, the ethnographic research I cited indicated that gang girls situationally "engag[ed] in presumptively masculine behaviors" (West and Zimmerman 1987, 139)—that is, "acting bad"—yet without jeopardizing or discrediting their fundamental gender project of "being a girl." Gang girls were engaging in a variety of practices that, no matter how much they may have contradicted conceptions of emphasized femininity, did not, in themselves, remove them from the category *girl*.

Thus, the ethnographic research I worked with indicated something quite different from what criminologists such as Freda Adler (1975, 1977) had argued—the majority of gang girls were not increasingly attempting to be masculine and, thus, embodying undifferentiated gender sameness. Rather, these girls engaged in physical violence authentically as girls and as an aspect of their femininity. More specifically, the intent of this paper was fourfold. First, although gang girls occasionally engaged in situationally defined masculine practices (physical violence), I argued against the position that the majority of gang girls were becoming "more masculine" and that this alleged increasing masculinity was the result of second-wave feminism (the Adler position). Second, the article suggested *one* route for criminology to possess the theoretical tools necessary to explain when girls and women as *girls and women* engaged in similar crimes as boys and men. Third, the article illuminated gender salience by examining both gender difference and gender similarity in the analysis of crime. And finally, the article demonstrated the fluidity of gender by showing that gang girls situationally defied emphasized femininity by "acting bad," yet without changing their overall fundamental gender project—they simply *disrupted difference by redefining what it means to be a girl.*

Arguably, Tina's case supports this position. Indeed, it is significant that Tina's practices of bodily empowerment at home and at school (engaging in assaultive violence) occurred contemporaneously with conspicuous displays and practices of femininity. In this regard, Tina is similar not only to the gang girls in the ethnographic studies reviewed in my 1995 paper, but also to third-wave feminists in the sense of dramatizing a seemingly incongruous relationship between feminine appearance and practices and public (as well as private) bodily empowerment (Messner 2000). Third-wave feminist literature of the mid- to late-1990s underscored that toughness and femininity are not mutually exclusive but, rather, are lived practices of the same reality (Heywood and Drake 1997; Messner 2000).[3] Third-wave feminists of the 1990s supported, for example, second-wave criticisms of beauty culture and power relations while simultaneously acknowledging and making use of the pleasures and defining potentialities of beauty and power. As Leslie Heywood and Jennifer Drake (1997, 8) point out in their introduction to *Third Wave Agenda*: "The lived messiness of the third wave is what defines it." Melissa Klein added that third-wave feminism moved away from a struggle for equality toward *disrupting difference* by asserting that girls can have the best of both worlds; for example, they can be both "violently angry" and "vampily glamorous" (1997, 208). Third-wave feminism differs from second-wave feminism in the way it is defined by contradictions and "grew not out of girls wanting sensitive boys so much as girls wanting to be tough girls" (Klein, 1997, 212). Klein (1997, 207) defined her feminism through bodily appearance and practice:

> I am twenty-five years old. On my left upper arm I have a six-inch-long tattoo of a voluptuous cowgirl. One of her hands rests jauntily on her jutting hip. The other is firing a gun. An earlier feminist might frown upon my cowgirl's fringed hot pants and halter top as promoting sexual exploitation, and might see her pistol as perpetuating male patterns of violence. Yet I see this image as distinctly feminist. Having a tattoo signifies a subculture that subverts traditional notions of feminine beauty. That this tattoo is a pinup girl with a gun represents the appropriation and redefinition of sexuality, power, and violence—ideas characteristic of third-wave punk feminism.

Much of third-wave feminism in the 1990s found its identity in popular music icons (for example, Courtney Love) who emphasized contradictions in both their lyrics and their gender appearance—such as glamorous and grunge, feminine and masculine, strong and weak, responsible and rebellious—and was manifest in punk and Riot Grrrl subcultures (Heywood and Drake 1997; Klein 1997). Thus, within the 1990s third-wave feminist movement, femininity and toughness were not simply consonant parts of one's self, they were a political imperative that *disrupted gender difference.* Moreover, a number of academic studies since the publication of my 1995 paper have shed light on girls' willingness to "act bad" or "tough" in feminine display without changing their fundamental gender project.

In an instructive conference paper, Debbie Archer (1995, 1) reported in the mid-1990s that in the United States as well as in England there had emerged a new type of femininity that was being displayed by young women. Archer did not examine the fluidity of gender but pointed to a particular street-girl "style" that found its articulation in certain music forms—such as hip-hop—as well as in Riot Grrrl subcultures. Archer (1995, 4) argued that these girls did not see themselves simply as "male 'clones'" (as Adler would have it), but rather as girls who "flaunt their difference and individuality as young women." For example, Archer described the "Peckham Girls" of South London—who are black, poor, live in inner-city housing estates, and do not attend school—in the following way: "They are 'flamboyantly dressed,' wearing gold sun visors, pink fluorescent leggings, red blouson jackets, baseball caps and lots of jewellery including nose studs, several earrings on each ear and rings on every finger. They also wear vivid blue or green contact lenses which contrasts strikingly with their dark Afro-Caribbean complexions" (Archer 1995, 4).

Similar to both Tina and the girls described in the ethnographic research I relied upon in my 1995 paper, Archer recounted that these girls aimed to be seen as women as well as being combative and capable of fighting to defend their own name, their group reputation, and their territory. As Archer stridently pointed out, these girls were constructing "an aggressive form of femininity" (1995, 6). Moreover, Archer also viewed hip-hop—such as the style and lyrics of Queen Latifah—as the voice of the street for, in particular, many African American and Latina girls, embodying "an angry rage against norms of femininity which they challenge by *calling themselves girls and by rewriting the word*, to show their rebellion and rage against traditional values" (1995, 9; my emphasis). In other words, they *redefined* what it means to be a girl by *disrupting* difference.

Archer concluded that for certain girls in the United States and England, "acting bad" while simultaneously dressing feminine are means of redefining "the norms and values of femininity . . . by asserting their independence in their actions and by finding their own cultural values, expressed through the way they live their lives on the street" (1995, 10).

Four years later, Natalie Adams (1999) published her qualitative research on middle school female adolescent fighting in the Deep South of the United States. Adams studied girls in junior high school and argued that in negotiating gender, these girls must engage in a type of sexual politics that concentrates on who will control their bodies and for what reasons. Her data showed that some girls recognize that physical strength, prowess, and aggressiveness are valued in U.S. society. Consequently, for these girls fighting becomes a legitimate avenue for gaining access to power. Adams viewed girls fighting as a *masculine metaphor* that resists the objectification and normalization of the "docile" female body. Indeed, a common phrase expressed by the girls in her study was that they "fight like a man." But their fighting also represents a struggle against reducing their body to a "thing." By engaging in fighting, girls gain entrance into a realm usually reserved for males—the informal, in-school system of persuasion, invincibility, and power. Consequently, their fighting "becomes *symbolic* of this struggle to move from no/*body* (an object) to some/*body* (a subject)" (Adams 1999, 128).

Critically, however, when Adams examined the substance of their fighting she found that girls' engagement in physical violence actually sustained the normalization of femininity. A contextual reading of why these girls fought, how they fought, under what circumstances they fought, and how they justify their fighting revealed to Adams that "acting bad" actually "validates what has traditionally been viewed as women's ways of knowing and making sense of the world through relationships and connections to others" (1999, 128). One of the primary reasons these girls fought was to prove their allegiance to a girlfriend that represented their subscription to emphasized femininity, underscoring selfless-ness, loyalty, and caring. Embedded in the girls' stories was an understanding of "respect" that transcended a masculine understanding of respect found in the street culture of boys as a personal and individual issue (Adams 1999, 129). For these girls, a relational understanding of respect was prevalent in which "respect for others is paramount in maintaining solid, stable relationships." Yet their fighting additionally reproduced femininity in another way—to either preserve or earn the position of someone's girlfriend. The girls adhered to an ideology of heterosexual monogamy and, thus, "messing" with someone's boyfriend vio-lated this monogamy and threatened one's security in "belonging" to a man. Thus, their fighting to gain or maintain such monogamy "affirm[ed] one's fem-ininity and value as a person" (Adams 1999, 130). Moreover, when Adams sug-gested to the girls that their aggressive behavior may be seen by others as ab-normal for girls (that is, attempting to be "one of the boys"), they grew quite indignant. The following are selected examples of the girls' responses:

> Sharon claimed that such interpretations are sexist. India added, "When I fight, I'm just handling my business. I ain't got no time to act like a boy. I'm a girl and I'm going to stay a girl for the rest of my life. I ain't like Michael Jackson [meaning her gendered self was not subject to being questioned]." And Sharon loudly an-nounced, "When I fight, I ain't trying to act like no boy; I'm just . . . being myself." (Adams 1999, 134–135)

And as Adams went on to point out:

> [These girls] do not view their fighting as unfeminine behavior. Quite the opposite— they perceive themselves to be very feminine. For these girls, asserting oneself (either physically or verbally) is not only appropriate behavior for both males and females but also a necessary survival tool. In fact, [the girls] view females who allow others to control them as not being "womanish" or "not being woman enough"; thus, to be silent or to become a victim of someone else's aggression is considered by them to be abnormal feminine behavior.

Adams's girls were not passively and uncritically accepting emphasized fem-ininity but, rather, they "appropriate[d] their own ideology of femininity and shape[d] it in ways that [made] sense in their lives" (Adams 1999, 131). Thus, these girls—like Tina—situationally "act bad" through fighting, yet do not change their fundamental gender project: what they do is *redefine* what it means to be a girl in their particular milieu by *disrupting* difference.

Consider also the recently published article by Karen Joe-Laidler and Geof-
frey Hunt (2001), who examined the meanings of femininity as they are understood and practiced by Latina, African American, and Asian-Pacific American
gang girls. Their analysis was based on interviews with 141 gang girls in the San
Francisco Bay Area and showed (similar to Adams's study) that the notion of
"respect" is highly gendered and holds a very different meaning for gang girls
than for gang boys. As Joe-Laidler and Hunt pointed out, for gang girls respect
is not understood solely in masculine street terms of power and control but,
rather, "is associated with the pursuit of respectability, one important dimension
of 'being feminine'" (2001, 664). Regardless of their ethnic and cultural background, respectability involves both physical appearance and social practice:
"Her clothing, hairstyle, make-up, and stride signify her status as a reputable
young woman. Yet her subtleness, restraint, and regards for others are also critical to distinguishing her from others" (Joe-Laidler and Hunt 2001, 664). Joe-
Laidler and Hunt examined respectability as it was negotiated and challenged in
a number of interactional settings—in the family and among gang girls and between gang girls and gang boys. In the family gang girls learned that a respectable woman does not "sleep around," does not get heavily involved in
drugs and alcohol, and she looks after her family. Specifically within the gang,
sexual reputation is at the core of their definition of respectability. Gang girls
construct sexually promiscuous girls as "Other," and this "Othering" reinforces
their own identity and investment in femininity, thereby strengthening solidarity
among gang members. Gang girls also engaged in "safe partying," whereby they
watched each other's backs while drinking and drugging, therefore protecting
each other from "risky situations." In interaction with gang boys, "the girls are
clearly aware of the importance of 'acting like a woman,' but also define how far
they are willing to do this, and refuse to give up their autonomy as individuals"
(Joe-Laidler and Hunt 2001, 675).

Regarding violence, Joe-Laidler and Hunt (2001, 670) asked: "How do we
account for this paradox between their aspirations of 'being young women' and
'being bad?'" They argued against the popular perception that gang girls were
attempting to "become 'macho' like their male counterparts," maintaining instead that these gang girls were more often "acting bad" rather than "being bad,"
thus helping to protect themselves in a patriarchal environment.[4] But "acting
bad" is also "a form of resistance to informal controls on their attempts to explore adolescence and femininity, and for demonstrating a sense of power in an
environment that provides them with little status. In this connection, gang girl
violence is also one of the very few resources for defending one's reputation as
respectable" (Joe-Laidler and Hunt 2001, 676).

Thus, for Joe-Laidler and Hunt, gang-girl femininity is tied not only to conventional practices of feminine respectability but, additionally: "Gang girls would hardly accept total submission to normative notions of femininity. Being a young woman does not mean sacrificing exploration and independence" (2001, 671–672). Gang girls do not "constantly engage in the construction of a 'badass' image. . . . The accomplishment of femininity occurs through interaction with others and is based in large part, but not exclusively, on acting and being respect(able)" (Joe-Laidler and Hunt 2001, 676).

Given the above studies that show violent girls constructing an assaultive gendered self that is *different* from other girls *and* from boys, we should not be surprised to read in the introductory chapter of a recent volume that includes a wide range of international studies on violent girls the suggestion that such girls are not attempting to be *more like boys* but, rather, are demonstrating their *difference* from boys (Alder and Worrall 2004). And in Laurie Schaffner's study of assaultive girls (2004), she found that girls are not "acting like boys," but are choosing to be both "sexy" and "aggressive." In other words, for many adolescent girls—both in and out of gangs—"acting bad," occasional masculine practices, and femininity are not incompatible.

The point of this discussion, then, is not to argue that assaultive adolescent girls are at the forefront of third-wave feminism—they are not—but to suggest that many of these girls (clearly not all) similarly appear to find consonance between toughness and femininity as part of the same lived reality—Tina is not alone—and therefore how girls *as girls* commit assaultive violence. Although engaging occasionally in masculine practices such as fighting, girls like Tina are *disrupting gender difference* through a redefining of what it means to be a girl by striving to boast a "bad-girl femininity."

A THIRD GENDER

This conclusion, however, in no way negates the fact that *some* girls construct a fundamental masculine gender project by in part displaying themselves in a masculine way, engaging primarily in what they and others in their milieu consider to be authentically masculine behavior, and outright rejecting most aspects of femininity. Indeed, this is the conclusion of Jody Miller (2001, 2002) who contends that the evidence presented in her book, *One of the Guys*, shows that certain gang girls identify with the boys in their gangs and describe such gangs as "masculinist enterprises": "To be sure, 'one of the guys' is only one part of a complex tapestry of gender beliefs and identities held by the gang girls

I spoke with—and is rarely matched by gendered actions—but it remains significant nonetheless" (Miller 2002, 442). Pointing out that gender inequality is rampant in the mixed-gender gangs of which these girls were members—such as male leadership, a double standard with regard to sexual activities, the sexual exploitation of some girls, and most girls' exclusion from serious gang crime—certain girls differentiated themselves from other girls through a construction of "one of the guys." In other words, the notion "one of the guys" is not fashioned by being *similar* to boys but, rather, certain girls being *different* from other girls.

Miller (2002, 442) employs a modified version of Thorne's (1993) notion of "gender crossing"—whereby gang girls who "cross" (join male-dominated, mixed-gender gangs) exclusively embrace a "masculine identity"—to explain how certain girls differentiate themselves from other girls:

> Even within their gangs, status hierarchies among girls were evident and dictated in part how successfully girls could resist gender typecasting and cross into boys' terrain. Clearly, part of what young women were doing was constructing an identity in opposition to other normative constructs of femininity. But they were "crossing" gender to do so. . . . These girls' accounts do not simply reflect the construction of a "bad-girl" femininity that is differentiated from other femininities; instead, they reflect gender crossing, embracing a *masculine* identity that they view as contradicting their bodily sex category (that is, female). (2002, 443)

Miller's research contributes to the process of discovering differences among gang girls, especially regarding how the distribution of male and female members within particular gangs may impact gender construction. Indeed, although I failed to distinguish different constructions of gender among gang girls in my 1995 paper, Miller's work helps point us in one direction for discovering these differences and how girls, like boys, can construct a masculine self.

Notwithstanding, the case of Kelly raises interesting questions regarding girls' constructions of a masculine self in certain settings and whether or not under relations of gender inequality girls actually can become "one of the guys." Although Kelly reported similar gender inequalities to those experienced by the gang girls Miller interviewed and similarly distanced herself from the "slutty badass girls," these inequalities ensured that Kelly's experience as a masculine badass-group member could never be the same as the boys' in that specific setting. This was particularly evident in the heterosexual meanings of the group, where Kelly experienced a dilemma about sexuality—she had to be asexual in that setting in order to sustain masculine accountability. Accordingly,

Kelly's masculine self was different qualitatively from that of the badass boys' as she did not do masculinity on the same bodily terms as the boys. This is not dissimilar to the girls in Miller's study. For example, Miller cited the following comment from "Latisha," one of the gang girls she interviewed: "We just like dudes to them [male gang members]. We just like dudes, they treat us like that 'cause we act so much like dudes they can't do nothing. *They respect us as females though*, but we just so much like dudes that they just don't trip off of it" (2002, 446).

Miller pointed out that Latisha's meaning of "respect" was "specifically that boys do not over-emphasize gender-marking and heterosexual meanings—they do not interact with girls who are 'one of the guys' in overly sexualized ways." Thus, like Kelly, the masculinity of Latisha and other "one of the guys" girls in Miller's study was *different* qualitatively (and could only be so) from the masculinity of the boys in the gang.

Moreover, Kelly was constituted as a different kind of group member because her body was subordinate in the sense of allegedly being unable to participate adequately in violence. For example, because Kelly did not "pass" as a "real" male, she was "allowed" to participate only in certain forms of group violence—those where the boys determined Kelly would not get in the way or be hurt (she was disallowed participation in *all* robberies and burglaries)—and this worked against her as a fully embodied and accountably masculine member of the group. In other words, Kelly was conceptualized as "unfeminine" but not "unfemale." Consequently, and although Kelly strove to "blend in" and to avoid bodily characteristics that might reinforce girl stereotyping—that is, she *attempted* to be accountably masculine—she still was seen by the boys as deficient in certain ways. Because gender power pervaded perceptions of individual performance in the badass group, the boys laid claim to what bodily characteristics were sufficiently accountable. Kelly behaved in broadly similar ways as the boys in the group (even participating in the power barfs!), attempting to replicate preexisting masculine norms. Despite her fighting ability and deemphasizing her gender difference, because she did not "pass" completely as male, the "real" male body remained the standard that positioned "unreal" female bodies as "out of place." In other words, Kelly's life story showed that what characteristics, practices, and bodies qualify as masculine is a political question. Accordingly, Kelly was subordinated and excluded from power in the group because she was not completely accountably masculine according to those with the power to make such a determination.

Consequently, although Kelly's embodied practices in the three milieus did not *erase* gender difference, they did *disrupt* it. Kelly's story raises a seminal question: If girls and women do not completely "pass" as "male," can they ever escape difference? Kelly clearly did not, as she was disallowed entrance into the same masculine *place* in gender relations as the badass boys. Thus, it is important to underline that drawing attention solely to differences among girls, and/or similarities between boys and girls, can make it difficult to understand how girls' (and women's) *collective* disadvantage may be institutionalized in particular settings, such as a teenage badass group. Indeed, even though Kelly engaged in masculine practices in the badass group, the constraints placed upon her resulted in Kelly most likely constituting a *third gender* in this particular setting—not "one of the guys." Let us now examine more carefully the intriguing possibility that Kelly's disruption of gender difference is not only significantly different from the case of Tina, but that Kelly indeed embodies a third gender in the specific setting of the badass group.

As discussed briefly in chapter 2, there are numerous cross-cultural examples of third and fourth genders in various societies. That is, certain individuals in specific times and places transcend the categories of "masculine" or "feminine," as they are understood in that particular society, and construct unique types of gender. For example, consider the traditional *berdache*[5] in the Klamath, Mohave, Maricopa, and Ciocopa Native American societies of western North America (Blackwood 1994). Anthropological research shows that in these societies certain girls avoided defined girl practices: they played with boys rather than with girls, and they participated in such boy tasks as making bows and arrows. Adults accepted this behavior among girls who chose it, and upon reaching puberty the girls would be recognized formally as berdache through specific ceremonies. As an adult, berdache women hunted, trapped, cultivated crops, fought in battles, and wore "male" clothing; that is, they were defined socially as constituting "social man with a vagina" (Bolin 1994). These women were under no obligation to bear children, indicating that societal emphasis was placed upon their interests and abilities, not their value as a producer (Blackwood 1994). Moreover, all of these societies permitted homosexual, premarital, and extramarital sexual relations, and berdache women often married nonberdache women: "A woman could follow the traditional female gender role, yet marry and make love with another woman without being stigmatized by such behavior" (Blackwood 1994, 306). Thus, the overall gender appearance and performance of berdache women combined a variety of masculine and feminine practices as well as unique activities specific to their gender (Roscoe 1998). Berdache women were accepted and integrated members of their communities who occupied an intermediate place—a third gender—in the particular gender relations embedded in these Native American societies.[6]

Berdache women provide evidence of the complicated and diverse nature of gender embodiment and move us beyond the Western masculine/feminine dichotomy toward the recognition of alternative gender dimensions. Indeed, this complexity and variety are likewise echoed in Kelly's gender appearance and practice, which disrupt the notion of only two oppositional gender categories, and like the berdache women, challenge perspectives that conflate sex and gender. Kelly's life story is somewhat analogous to berdache women in the sense that during early childhood she engaged mostly in what she called "boyish" behavior—eventually embodying a complicit, in-home (albeit subordinate) masculinity—and within the settings of school and the badass group she combined masculine and feminine appearance and practices. Although clearly embodying a masculine *presence*, yet also rejected by her peers at school, the boys and girls in the badass group recognized her uniqueness by referring to Kelly as "ladybug" (because male and female ladybugs look the same and perform the same activities) and fully accepted and integrated her into the group. Kelly of course did not enjoy the gender and sexual equality that berdache women relished—as noted, she had to remain asexual in the badass setting and her body was subordinated to the "male body"—yet through her agency she nevertheless carved out a special embodied niche. Like berdache women, Kelly steered an intermediate course in the badass-group context, interacting with and through her body as both masculine and feminine. Kelly appeared as a *gender blend*, cultivating an embodied androgynous self that defied the embodiment of girls like Tina as well as badass boys. Kelly constituted a different type of embodiment—*a social boy with a vagina*—and therefore a unique and intermediate *place* within the gender relations of the badass group. Kelly *disrupted* gender difference by approximating a boy but not fully becoming a boy; she embodied a gender neither masculine nor feminine, but situationally a novel combination—a third gender.

Such embodiments exist in Western societies (not simply in traditional Native American societies) but rarely are recognized. Cases in point are those who label themselves *transgender*, an umbrella term designating people who "traverse, bridge, or blur the boundary of the *gender expression* they were assigned at birth" (Feinberg 1996, x). Both *transgenderists* and *transsexuals* are members of the transgender community. However, a transgenderist is different from a transsexual in the sense that a preoperative transsexual attempts to *pass* as the "other gender," whereas a postoperative transsexual actually *becomes* the "other sex." As the language just used suggests, then, transsexuals sustain the Western binary that equates sex with gender. The transgenderist is different by living an androgynous "blend" without surgical reassignment and suggests that gender exists on a continuum rather than in opposition (Bolin 1994). The transgenderist is the "self-proclaimed androgyne, the individual who wishes to express both male and female identification through sartorial and bodily symbols of gender, appearing as a blend, sometimes of one gender more than the other" (Bolin 1994, 466). Thus, like a transgenderist, Kelly "reiterates what the cross-cultural record reveals: the independence of gender traits embodied in a biocentric model of sex" (Bolin 1994, 448).[7]

Not surprisingly, then, what the evidence on Tina and Kelly (as well as other assaultive girls and boys) suggests is *gender diversity* rather than *gender dichotomy*, as well as the need for further research to uncover not only more data on that gender variety but its relation to crime and violence. Consequently, and because we are left with numerous questions in search of answers, I recommend the following for criminological consideration specifically regarding assaultive girls: Which girls "do" femininity, which "do" masculinity, and which "do" third (fourth, and so on) gender, and why? What are the specific circumstances for embodying different forms of gender? How are these different gender types related to crime and violence? For those girls who embody a masculine self, how is their masculinity different from and similar to the masculinity embodied by boys in their particular milieus? And when are gender, race, class, age, and sexuality salient to the commission of crime by girls? In short, although early second-wave feminist criminologists successfully replaced corporeal woman with gendered woman (and social man with gendered man), perhaps the task of current criminological scholars will be to not only further "embody criminology" but to additionally "deconstruct" the mind–body, sex–gender, and gender difference binaries.

Structured action theory has a long-established emphasis on the salience and fluidity of gender (as well as of race, class, age, and sexuality) and, therefore, offers *one* theoretical model for exploring the above questions as well as these new frontiers. Structured action theory acknowledges that both boys and girls are capable of "doing" masculinities and femininities as well as other forms of gender embodiment. What is essential for understanding these various forms of gender construction and their relation to crime, however, is conceptualizing *how* embodied social action is structured by specific gender relations (as well as by race, age, class, and sexuality) within particular social settings.

NOTES

CHAPTER 1

1. According to Beirne (1993, 227), Beccaria more precisely argued for a "notion of human agency simultaneously involving free rational calculation and determined action."

2. Despite Foucault's substantial help in understanding the relationship between the body and the rise of what Garland (1994, 18) refers to as the "government project" in criminology (criminologists doing research in the service of the state), Foucault's view of the body is problematic (see chapter 2), as is his argument that punishment is solely a political instrument of control (see Garland 1990, 157–75 for an excellent critique of Foucault on punishment).

3. This is a new and complete translation of the text that first appeared in English as *The Female Offender*. The original Italian publication consisted of four major parts, but *The Female Offender* translated only one full part and small portions of another from the original (see Rafter and Gibson 2004).

4. Sutherland (1947) also devoted much time to criticizing the "body type" theorists, such as Hooton (1939a, b) and Sheldon (1949).

5. It must be noted, however, that Sutherland discussed (albeit briefly) how criminal acts are practices by embodied people in copresent interactions. For example, Sutherland (1924, 180; 1947, 93) consistently argued in his textbook that certain youth with "physiological defects"—such as crossed eyes and an unusually small or large body—may be ridiculed at school, eventually ostracized by law-abiding groups, and thereby "forced into" association with "antisocial groups." Thus, Sutherland not only rejected any notion of criminal acts as preprogrammed in the bodies of individual offenders, he also hinted at some youthful offenders being motivated to engage in crime through experiences with their bodies and through the way their bodies were received and treated by peers. Nevertheless, Sutherland never formally included agency

as embodied interaction in differential association theory and, thus, clearly became the most influential figure in inaugurating a disembodied, dualist, sociological criminology.

CHAPTER 2

1. Some sociological criminologists have integrated biology into their theoretical frameworks, but not *embodiment* or the *lived body* as a necessary and mediate component of social action. For example, in both social control (Hirschi 1969) and self-control (Gottfredson and Hirschi 1990) theories, there is a built-in assumption that antisocial tendencies are naturalized in the body and actualized only if various sorts of social control are relaxed or the individual does not learn self-control. These "control" ideas appear rooted in Christian notions that view the body as sinful and in need of strict regulation by the mind. Later in this chapter, I criticize conceptions of the "natural" body.

2. My book *Masculinities and Crime* (1993) likewise can be criticized for contributing to both a disembodied and gender-difference approach, as it completely ignores the body as well as the fact that girls and women sometimes engage in masculine practices and "male crime."

3. This now is beginning to change, as certain recent feminist criminological works examine girls and violence (Alder and Worrall 2004; Burman, Brown, Batchelor 2003; and Miller 2001).

4. See also the recent argument by Anthony Walsh (2002, 195–220) who miraculously proclaims that his "biosocial criminology" is compatible with feminist explanations of crime!

CHAPTER 3

1. "Assaultive violence" is defined as an attack by one person upon another for the purpose of inflicting physical pain and/or bodily injury. "Nonviolence" is defined as refraining from practicing assaultive violence.

2. I use the concepts "practice" and "social action" interchangeably, representing behavior that is simultaneously mindful and physical—that is, embodied.

CHAPTER 4

1. Exceptions are the important work of Mark Totten (2000), Michele Burman, Jane Brown, and Susan Batchelor (2003), and various chapters found in Christine Alder's and Anne Worrall's (2004) recently edited volume on violent girls.

2. The original sample also includes ten adolescent male and female sex offenders and ten adolescent male and female exclusively nonviolent individuals. However, none of their life stories are reported and analyzed in this book. The reason for their exclusion centers on the fact that comparison of their life stories and ultimate sexual offending and nonviolent behavior requires more time to analyze the particular data and I did not want to delay the publication of the currently included material. I will, of course, report my findings concerning the ten sex offenders and the ten nonviolent adolescents in a separate and future publication.

3. The method is a modified version of Jean-Paul Sartre's "existential psychoanalysis." For further discussion of existential psychoanalysis see Sartre (1956, 712–34) and Connell (1987, 211–17), and see Plummer (2001) for the breadth of coverage that the life-history method offers.

4. Shockingly, for girls involved in assaultive violence, I was unable to find even one girl who came from a nonviolent household.

5. Because of the in-depth and complex quality of the interviews, in part III, I report only four of the ten assaultive life stories. In the overall sample of assaultive offenders (ten), sex offenders (ten), and nonviolent youth (ten), I rejected one interview (a male sex offender) because of continual inconsistencies (I learned later this interviewee was severely medicated) and another interview because the boy (also a sex offender) was unable to discuss further his past relationship with his father (he broke down crying). The remaining six interviews of assaultive boys and girls are not reported in this book because of what is referred to in the literature as a "saturation-of-information" effect (Seidman 1998, 48). In other words, during the data analysis I reached a point where I began to find strikingly similar types of information being reported—I was no longer hearing anything "new." Therefore, these six stories are additionally not part of the discussion because they added nothing new to the data and would have produced only repetition. Moreover, I do not discuss how the respondents were caught, as this information could reveal their identity. Finally, my selection of white, working-class boys and girls limits any generalization to racial minority working-class youth as well as to middle-class youth. Clearly, there is a need for life-history research on these latter two categories of boys and girls.

6. Both the boys and girls initially appeared somewhat embarrassed and uncomfortable talking about any past physical and/or sexual abuse. However, all who experienced such abuse eventually did discuss the abusive events without any significant impairment. Surprisingly, the only major breakdown during an interview occurred when a boy was unable to continue discussing his relationship with his father (as pointed out in note 16), and the conversation was terminated.

CHAPTER 6

1. This may seem like a contradiction to Kelly's earlier statement that her mother "hardly did what he [stepfather] wanted." However, what Kelly referred to here is the fact

that Kelly's mother did what the stepfather demanded to avoid a beating or after being beaten. In other words, Kelly's mother would resist by "getting drunk" and not do "what he wanted," but that opposition was short-term, as eventually she would understandably submit—without defying him in any way—to his demands.

2. Kelly was also much different from Tina in that, as she states, "I never liked girls' magazines or really anything like that. I just liked to play sports and watch sports, you know." Thus, Kelly seems to have successfully resisted media and in-school pressure to be "a girl" in appearance and practice.

CHAPTER 7

1. There exists in the masculine culture of cruelty an important distinction between "bullying" and "fighting." For Perry and his friends, it was perfectly legitimate and therefore accountably masculine for them to "smack a kid in the face" so as to make him "look like a fool" in class. However, it was considered unmasculine to actually engage in a "fist fight" with a "wimp" because such a person was not much of a masculine challenge. This explains numerous student reactions to Lenny to "[p]ick on someone [his] own size."

CHAPTER 8

1. An analogous noncriminal example is women participating in "Roller Derby," in which women unite with men as team members engaging in similar physically aggressive masculine practices yet are assessed successfully by team members and by the viewing public as physically aggressive *women*.

2. Joe-Laidler and Hunt (2001, 659) recently summarized much of this same ethnographic research and built their examination of gang-girl femininity on conceptualization of the "bad girl."

3. For discussions of third-wave feminism, see Walker (1995), Heywood and Drake (1997), Baumgardner and Richards (2000), and Messner (2000).

4. Maher (1997, 95–96) likewise records this distinction between "acting bad" and "being bad" in her important work on women in the street-level drug economy.

5. The term *berdache* has been questioned by some scholars as a Western derogatory linguistic invention, but Roscoe (1998, 16–19) presents a convincing argument for retaining its use.

6. In nearly every Native American society with documented female berdache, male berdache are also present. When the same term is used to identify both male and female berdache, they belong to a third gender; when distinct terms are used, male berdache represent a third gender and female berdache a fourth gender (Roscoe 1998).

7. In a recent discussion of "crime and embodiment," Victoria Pitts (2003) argues that women and girls are often "disciplined" by society-wide discourses to create a body surface that supports emphasized femininity, but also that some girls and women resist

such discipline by engaging in, for example, deviant body modification (e.g., scarification). Thus, Pitts emphasizes the alteration of the body surface in which new (albeit dissident) meanings are inscribed. Although an interesting discussion, what is missing from her analysis are what Tina's and Kelly's life stories highlight: the situational social processes and practices through which the body becomes meaningful as violent or deviant. That is, how one interacts with and through the body in everyday life disappears in Pitts's analysis, thus forgoing any conceptualization of how crime and violence are actually embodied. Finally, although both girls' bodies were "disciplined" according to a "male gaze"—albeit differently since Tina looked "hot" to attract heterosexual boys while Kelly looked "tough" to be accepted by badass boys—that gaze is found almost exclusively at the local level of interaction rather than in broader discursive representations.

REFERENCES

Adams, N. G. 1999. "Fighting to Be Somebody: Resisting Erasure and the Discursive Practices of Female Adolescent Fighting." *Educational Studies* 30 (2): 115–39.

Adler, F. 1975. *Sisters in Crime*. New York: McGraw-Hill.

———. 1977. "The Interaction between Women's Emancipation and Female Criminality: A Cross-Cultural Perspective." *International Journal of Criminology and Penology* 5 (1): 101–12.

Agnew, R. 1990. "The Origins of Delinquent Events: An Examination of Offender Accounts." *Journal of Research in Crime and Delinquency* 27 (3): 267–94.

———. 1992. "Foundation for a General Strain Theory of Crime and Delinquency." *Criminology* 30 (1): 47–87.

———. 2001. "An Overview of General Strain Theory." In *Explaining Criminals and Crime: Essays in Contemporary Criminological Theory*, ed. R. Paternoster and R. Bachman, 161–74. Los Angeles: Roxbury.

Alder, C., and K. Polk. 1996. "Masculinity and Child Homicide." *British Journal of Criminology* 36 (3): 396–411.

Alder, C., and A. Worrall. 2004. "A Contemporary Crisis?" In *Girls' Violence: Myths and Realities*, ed. C. Alder and A. Worrall, 1–20. Albany: State University of New York Press.

Allen, J. 1989. "Men, Crime, and Criminology: Recasting the Questions." *International Journal of the Sociology of Law* 17 (1): 19–39.

Andersen, M. L. 1993. "Studying across Difference: Race, Class, and Gender in Qualitative Research." In *Race and Ethnicity in Research Methods*, ed. J. H. Stanfield and R. M. Dennis, 39–52. Newbury Park, Calif.: Sage.

Archer, D. 1995. "Riot Grrrl and Raisin Girl: Femininity within the Female Gang: The Power of the Popular." Paper presented at the British Criminology Conference, Loughborough University, July 18–21.

Assiter, A. 1996. *Enlightened Women: Modern Feminism in a Postmodern Age*. New York: Routledge.

Baumgardner, J., and A. Richards. 2000. *Manifesta: Young Women, Feminism, and the Future*. New York: Farrar, Straus and Giroux.

Beirne, P. 1993. *Inventing Criminology: Essays on the Rise of* Homo Criminalis. Albany: State University of New York Press.

Bartky, S. L. 1998. "Foucault, Femininity, and the Modernization of Patriarchal Power." In *The Politics of Women's Bodies: Sexuality, Appearance, and Behavior*, ed. R. Weitz, 25–45. New York: Oxford University Press.

Beccaria, C. 1764 (1963). *Of Crimes and Punishments*. Trans. Henry Paolucci. Indianapolis, Ind.: Bobbs-Merril.

Belknap, J. 2000. *The Invisible Woman: Gender, Crime, and Justice*. Belmont, Calif.: Wadsworth.

Bentham, J. 1780 (1973). *Introduction to the Principles of Morals and Legislation*. New York: Hafner Press.

Blackwood, E. 1994. "Sexuality and Gender in Certain Native American Tribes: The Case of Cross-Gender Females." In *Theorizing Feminism*, ed. A. C. Herrmann and A. J. Stewart, 301–15. Boulder, Colo.: Westview Press.

Bolin, A. 1994. "Transcending and Transgendering: Male-to-Female Transsexuals, Dichotomy and Diversity." In *Third Sex, Third Gender: Beyond Sexual Dimorphism in Culture and History*, ed. G. Herdt, 447–86. New York: Zone Books.

Bowker, L., ed. 1998. *Masculinities and Violence*. Thousand Oaks, Calif.: Sage.

Bowring, J. 1962. *The Works of Jeremy Bentham*. Vol. 4. New York: Russell and Russell.

Burman, M. 2004. "Turbulent Talk: Girls Making Sense of Violence." In *Girls' Violence*, ed. C. Alder and A. Worrall, 81–104. Albany: State University of New York Press.

Burman, M., J. Brown, and S. Batchelor. 2003. "'Taking it to Heart': Girls and the Meanings of Violence." In *The Meanings of Violence*, ed. E. A. Stanko, 71–89. New York: Routledge.

Burman, M., S. Batchelor, and J. Brown. 2001. "Researching Girls and Violence: Facing the Dilemmas of Fieldwork." *British Journal of Criminology* 41 (3): 443–59.

Cahill, S. E. 1986. "Childhood Socialization as a Recruitment Process: Some Lessons from the Study of Gender Development." In *Sociological Studies of Child Development*, ed. P. A. Adler and P. Adler, 163–86. Greenwich, Conn.: JAI Press.

Campbell, A. 1991. *The Girls in the Gang*. 2nd ed. Cambridge, Mass.: Basil Blackwell.

———. 1993. *Men, Women, and Aggression*. New York: Basic Books.

Canaan, J. 1987. "A Comparative Analysis of Middle School and High School Teenage Cliques." In *Interpretive Ethnography of Education*, ed. G. Spindler and L. Spindler, 385–406. Hillsdale, N.J.: Lawrence Erlbaum.

———. 1998. "Is 'Doing Nothing' Just Boys' Play? Integrating Feminist and Cultural Studies Perspectives on Working-Class Young Men's Masculinity." In *Criminology at the Crossroads: Feminist Readings in Crime and Justice*, ed. K. Daly and L. Maher, 172–87. New York: Oxford University Press.

Carlen, P., and T. Jefferson. 1996. Special issue, *British Journal of Criminology, Masculinities and Crime* 33 (6).

Chambliss, W. J. 1972. *The Box Man: A Professional Thief's Journey.* New York: Harper & Row.

Chesney-Lind, M., and J. Hagedorn, eds. 1999. *Female Gangs in America.* Chicago: Lake View Press.

Chesney-Lind, M., and L. Pasko. 2004. *The Female Offender: Girls, Women, and Crime.* 2nd ed. Thousand Oaks, Calif.: Sage.

Collier, R. 1998. *Masculinities, Crime and Criminology: Men, Heterosexuality and the Criminal(ised) Other.* London: Sage.

Collison, M. 1996. "In Search of the High Life: Drugs, Crime, Masculinities." *British Journal of Criminology* 36 (3): 428–44.

Connell, R. W. 1987. *Gender and Power: Society, the Person, and Sexual Politics.* Stanford, Calif.: Stanford University Press.

———. 1991. "Live Fast and Die Young: The Construction of Masculinity among Young Working-Class Men on the Margin of the Labour Market." *Australian and New Zealand Journal of Sociology* 27 (2): 141–71.

———. 1995. *Masculinities.* Berkeley: University of California Press.

———. 1996. "Teaching the Boys: New Research on Masculinity and Gender Strategies for Schools." *Teachers College Record* 98 (2): 206–35.

———. 1997a. "Comment on Hawkesworth's 'Confounding Gender': Re-structuring Gender." *Signs: Journal of Women in Culture and Society* 22 (3): 702–7.

———. 1997b. "Why is Classical Theory Classical?" *American Journal of Sociology* 102 (6): 1511–57.

———. 1998. "Making Gendered People: Bodies, Identities, Sexualities." In *Revisioning Gender,* ed. M. M. Ferree, J. Lorber, and B. B. Hess, 449–71. Thousand Oaks, Calif.: Sage.

———. 2000. *The Men and the Boys.* Sydney: Allen and Unwin.

———. 2002a. *Gender.* Cambridge: Polity Press.

———. 2002b. "On Hegemonic Masculinity and Violence: Response to Jefferson and Hall." *Theoretical Criminology* 6 (1): 89–99.

Crossley, N. 1995. "Body Techniques, Agency and Intercorporeality: On Goffman's *Relations in Public.*" *Sociology* 29 (1): 133–49.

———. 2001. *The Social Body: Habit, Identity and Desire.* Thousand Oaks, Calif.: Sage.

Daly, K. 1997. "Different Ways of Conceptualizing Sex/Gender in Feminist Theory and Their Implications for Criminology." *Theoretical Criminology* 1 (1): 25–53.

Daly, K., and M. Chesney-Lind. 1988. "Feminism and Criminology." *Justice Quarterly* 5 (4): 497–538.

Daly, K., and L. Maher, eds. 1998. *Criminology at the Crossroads: Feminist Readings in Crime and Justice.* New York: Oxford University Press.

Davis, K. 1997. "Embody-ing Theory: Beyond Modernist and Postmodernist Readings of the Body." In *Embodied Practices: Feminist Perspectives on the Body,* ed. K. Davis, 1–23. Thousand Oaks, Calif.: Sage.

de Beauvoir, S. 1972 (1949). *The Second Sex*. New York: Penguin.

Dowsett, G. W. 1996. *Practicing Desire: Homosexual Sex in the Era of Aids*. Stanford, Calif.: Stanford University Press.

Eckert, P. 1989. *Jocks and Burnouts: Social Categories and Identity in the High School*. New York: Teachers College Press, Columbia University.

Faith, K. 1993. *Unruly Women*. Vancouver: Press Gang Publishers.

Feinberg, L. 1996. *Transgender Warriors: Making History from Joan of Arc to Dennis Rodman*. Boston: Beacon Press.

Fenstermaker, S., and C. West, eds. 2002. *Doing Gender, Doing Difference*. New York: Routledge.

Ferguson, A. 1991. *Sexual Democracy: Women, Oppression, and Revolution*. Boulder, Colo.: Westview Press.

Foley, D. E. 1990. *Learning Capitalist Culture: Deep in the Heart of Tejas*. Philadelphia: University of Pennsylvania Press.

Foucault, M. 1979. *Discipline and Punish: The Birth of the Prison*. New York: Pantheon.

Garfinkel, H. 1967. *Studies in Ethnomethodology*. Englewood Cliffs, N.J.: Prentice-Hall.

Garland, D. 1990. *Punishment and Modern Society: A Study in Social Theory*. Chicago: University of Chicago Press.

——. 1994. "Of Crimes and Criminals: The Development of Criminology in Britain." In *The Oxford Handbook of Criminology*, ed. M. Maguire, R. Morgan, and R. Reiner, 17–68. Oxford: Clarendon.

Gaylord, M. S., and J. F. Galliher. 1988. *The Criminology of Edwin Sutherland*. New Brunswick, N.J.: Transaction Books.

Giddens, A. 1976. *New Rules of Sociological Method: A Positive Critique of Interpretive Sociologies*. New York: Basic Books.

——. 1981. "Agency, Institution, and Time-Space Analysis." In *Advances in Social Theory and Methodology: Toward an Integration of Micro- and Macro-Sociologies*, ed. K. Knorr-Cetina and A.V. Cicourel, 161–74. Boston: Routledge.

——. 1984. *The Constitution of Society*. Berkeley: University of California Press.

——. 1989. "A Reply to My Critics." In *Social Theories of Modern Societies: Anthony Giddens and His Critics*, ed. D. Held and J. B. Thompson, 249–30. New York: Cambridge University Press.

——. 1991. *Modernity and Self-Identity*. Stanford, Calif.: Stanford University Press.

Gilmore, D. D. 1990. *Manhood in the Making*. New Haven, Conn.: Yale University Press.

Glenn, E. N. 1992. "From Servitude to Service Work: Historical Continuities in the Racial Division of Paid Labor." *Signs: Journal of Women in Culture and Society* 18 (1): 1–43.

Glueck, S., and E. Glueck. 1934. *Five Hundred Delinquent Women*. New York: Knopf.

Goetting, A. 1999. *Getting Out: Life Stories of Women Who Left Abusive Men*. New York: Columbia University Press.

Goffman, E. 1963. *Behavior in Public Places*. New York: Free Press.

——. 1968. *Stigma*. Englewood Cliffs, N.J.: Prentice-Hall.

——. 1972. *Relations in Public*. New York: Harper & Row.

——. 1979. *Gender Advertisements*. New York: Harper & Row.

Gottfredson, M. R., and T. Hirschi. 1990. *A General Theory of Crime*. Stanford, Calif.: Stanford University Press.

Grosz, E. 1994. *Volatile Bodies: Toward a Corporeal Feminism*. Bloomington: Indiana University Press.

——. 1995. *Space, Time, and Perversion: Essays on the Politics of the Body*. New York: Routledge.

Hagan, J. 1989. *Structural Criminology*. New Brunswick, N.J.: Rutgers University Press.

Hagan, J., B. McCarthy, and H. Foster. 2002. "A Gendered Theory of Delinquency and Despair in the Life Course." *Acta Sociologica* 45: 37–46.

Hagedorn, J. 1998. "Frat Boys, Bossman, Studs, and Gentlemen." In *Masculinities and Violence*, ed. L. Bowker, 201–22. Thousand Oaks, Calif.: Sage.

Herdt, G. 1994. "Mistaken Sex: Culture, Biology and the Third Sex in New Guinea." In *Third Sex, Third Gender: Beyond Sexual Dimorphism in Culture and History*, ed. G. Herdt, 419–445. New York: Zone Books.

Heritier-Auge, F. 1989. "Older Women, Stout-Hearted Women, Women of Substance." In *Fragments for a History of the Human Body*, ed. M. Feher, R. Naddaff, and N. Tazi, part III, 281–99. New York: Zone Books.

Heywood, L., and J. Drake. 1997. "Introduction." In *Third Wave Agenda: Being Feminist, Doing Feminism*, ed. L. Heywood and J. Drake, 1–20. Minneapolis: University of Minnesota Press.

Hirschi, T. 1969. *Causes of Delinquency*. Berkeley, Calif.: University of California Press.

Hobbs, D. 1995. *Bad Business: Professional Crime in Modern Britain*. New York: Oxford University Press.

Holstein, J. A., and J. F. Gubrium. 1995. *The Active Interview*. Thousand Oaks, Calif.: Sage.

Hood-Williams, J. 2001. "Gender, Masculinities and Crime: From Structures to Psyches." *Theoretical Criminology* 5 (1): 37–60.

Hooton, E. A. 1939a. *Crime and the Man*. Cambridge, Mass.: Harvard University Press.

——. 1939b. *The American Criminal*. Cambridge, Mass.: Harvard University Press.

Horn, D. 2003. *The Criminal Body: Lombroso and the Anatomy of Deviance*. New York: Routledge.

Joe-Laidler, K., and G. Hunt. 2001. "Accomplishing Femininity among the Girls in the Gang." *British Journal of Criminology* 41: 656–78.

Kaplan, G. T., and L. J. Rogers. 1990. "The Definition of Male and Female: Biological Reductionism and the Sanctions of Normality." In *Feminist Knowledge: Critique and Construct*, ed. S. Gunew, 205–228. New York: Routledge.

Kessler, S. 1990. "The Medical Construction of Gender: Case Management of Intersexed Infants." *Signs: Journal of Women in Culture and Society* 16 (1): 3–26.

Kessler, S., and W. McKenna. 1978. *Gender: An Ethnomethodological Approach*. New York: John Wiley.

Kimmel, M. S., and M. Mahler. 2003. "Adolescent Masculinity, Homophobia, and Violence: Random School Shootings, 1982–2001." *American Behavioral Scientist* 46 (10): 1439–58.

Kindlon, D., and M. Thompson. 1999. *Raising Cain: Protecting the Emotional Life of Boys.* New York: Ballantine.

Klein, M. 1997. "Duality and Redefinition: Young Feminism and the Alternative Music Community." In *Third Wave Agenda: Being Feminist, Doing Feminism*, ed. L. Heywood and J. Drake, 207–25. Minneapolis: University of Minnesota Press.

Kobrin, S. 1982. "The Uses of the Life-History Document for the Development of Delinquency Theory." In *The Jack Roller at Seventy*, ed. J. Snodgrass, 153–65. Lexington, Mass.: Lexington Books.

Laub, J. H., and R. J. Sampson. 1991. "The Sutherland–Glueck Debate: On the Sociology of Criminological Knowledge." *American Journal of Sociology* 96 (6): 1402–40.

Laqueur, T. 1990. *Making Sex: Body and Gender from the Greeks to Freud.* Cambridge, Mass.: Harvard University Press.

Lefkowitz, B. 1997. *Our Guys: The Glen Ridge Rape and the Secret Life of the Perfect Suburb.* Berkeley: University of California Press.

Leonard, E. B. 1982. *Women, Crime, and Society: A Critique of Criminological Theory.* New York: Longman.

Lombroso, C. 1876. *L'Uomo delinquente.* Milan: Hoepl.

Lombroso, C., and G. Ferrero. 1893 (2004). *Criminal Woman, the Prostitute, and the Normal Woman.* Trans. N. H. Rafter and M. Gibson. Durham, N.C.: Duke University Press.

Lorber, J. 1994. *Paradoxes of Gender.* New Haven, Conn.: Yale University Press.

Maher, L. 1997. *Sexed Work: Gender, Race, and Resistance in a Brooklyn Drug Market.* New York: Oxford University Press.

Martin, K. A. 1996. *Puberty, Sexuality, and the Self: Boys and Girls at Adolescence.* New York: Routledge.

——. 1998. "Becoming a Gendered Body: Practices of Preschools." *American Sociological Review* 63 (August): 494–511.

Martin, M. K., and B. Voorhies. 1975. *Female of the Species.* New York: Columbia University Press.

Martin, S. E., and N. C. Jurik. 1996. *Doing Justice, Doing Gender: Women in Law and Criminal Justice Occupations.* Thousand Oaks, Calif.: Sage.

Messerschmidt, J. W. 1993. *Masculinities and Crime: Critique and Reconceptualization of Theory.* Lanham, Md.: Rowman & Littlefield.

——. 1995. "From Patriarchy to Gender: Feminist Theory, Criminology, and the Challenge of Diversity." In *International Feminist Perspectives in Criminology*, ed. N. H. Rafter and F. Heidensohn, 167–88. Philadelphia: Open University Press.

——. 1997. *Crime as Structured Action: Gender, Race, Class, and Crime in the Making.* Thousand Oaks, Calif.: Sage.

———. 2000. *Nine Lives: Adolescent Masculinities, the Body, and Violence*. Boulder, Colo.: Westview Press.

Messner, M. 1992. *Power at Play: Sports and the Problem of Masculinity*. Boston: Beacon Press.

———. 2000. "Barbie Girls versus Sea Monsters: Children Constructing Gender." *Gender & Society* 14 (6): 765–84.

Miller, J. 2001. *One of the Guys: Girls, Gangs, and Gender*. New York: Oxford University Press.

———. 2002. "The Strengths and Limits of 'Doing Gender' for Understanding Street Crime." *Theoretical Criminology* 6 (4): 433–60.

Morgan, D. 1992. *Discovering Men*. New York: Routledge.

Morgan, D., and S. Scott, eds. 1993. *Body Matters: Essays on the Sociology of the Body*. Washington, D.C.: Falmer Press.

Naffine, N. 1987. *Female Crime: The Construction of Women in Criminology*. Sydney: Allen and Unwin.

———, ed. 1995. *Gender, Crime, and Feminism*. Brookfield, Mass.: Dartmouth Publishing Company.

Nanda, S. 1990. *Neither Man nor Woman: The Hijiras of India*. Belmont, Calif.: Wadsworth.

Newburn, T., and E. A. Stanko, eds. 1994. *Just Boys Doing Business? Men, Masculinities and Crime*. London: Routledge.

Oakley, A. 1972. *Sex, Gender and Society*. San Francisco: Harper and Row.

———. 1997. "A Brief History of Gender." In *Who's Afraid of Feminism? Seeing through the Backlash*, ed. A. Oakley and J. Mitchell, 29–55. New York: New Press.

Orbuch, T. 1997. "People's Accounts Count: The Sociology of Accounts." In *Annual Review of Sociology*, vol. 23, J. Hagan and K. S. Cook, 455–78. Palo Alto, Calif.: Annual Reviews.

Oudshoorn, N. 1994. *Beyond the Natural Body: An Archaeology of Sex Hormones*. New York: Routledge.

Padfield, M., and I. Procter. 1996. "The Effect of Interviewer's Gender on the Interviewing Process: A Comparative Study." *Sociology* 30 (2): 355–66.

Patton, M. Q. 1990. *Qualitative Evaluation and Research Methods*. Newbury Park, Calif.: Sage.

Petersen, A. C. 1988. "Adolescent Development." *Annual Review of Psychology* 39: 583–607.

Pitts, V. 2003. "Crime and Embodiment." In *Controversies in Critical Criminology*, ed. M. D. Schwartz and S. E. Hatty, 121–31. Cincinnati, Ohio: Anderson.

Plummer, K. 2001. *Documents of Life II: An Invitation to a Critical Humanism*. Thousand Oaks, Calif.: Sage.

Polk, K. 1994. *When Men Kill: Scenarios of Masculine Violence*. New York: Cambridge University Press.

Pollak, O. 1950. *The Criminality of Women*. New York: A. S. Barnes.

Rafter, N. H., and M. Gibson. 2004. "Editors' Introduction." In *Criminal Woman, the Prostitute, and the Normal Woman*, ed. C. Lombroso and G. Ferrero, 3–33. Durham, N.C.: Duke University Press.

Rafter, N. H., and F. Heidensohn. 1995. "Introduction: The Development of Feminist Perspectives on Crime." In *International Feminist Perspectives in Criminology: Engendering a Discipline*, ed. N. H. Rafter and F. Heidensohn, 1–14. Philadelphia: Open University Press.

Reinhartz, S. 1992. *Feminist Methods in Social Research*. New York: Oxford University Press.

Richardson, L. 1990. *Writing Strategies: Reaching Diverse Audiences*. Newbury Park, Calif.: Sage.

Roscoe, W. 1998. *Changing Ones: Third and Fourth Genders in Native North America*. New York: St. Martins Press.

Rowe, D. 2002. *Biology and Crime*. Los Angeles: Roxbury.

Sabo, D., T. A. Kupers, and W. London, eds. 2001. *Prison Masculinities*. Philadelphia: Temple University Press.

Sampson, R. J., and J. H. Laub. 1993. *Crime in the Making: Pathways and Turning Points through Life*. Cambridge, Mass.: Harvard University Press.

Sartre, J. P. 1956. *Being and Nothingness*. New York: Washington Square Press.

———. 1963. *Search for a Method*. New York: Alfred A. Knopf.

Seidman, I. 1998. *Interviewing as Qualitative Research*. New York: Teachers College Press, Columbia University.

Schaffner, L. 2004. "Capturing Girls' Experiences of 'Community Violence' in the United States." In *Girls' Violence: Myths and Realities*, ed. C. Alder and A. Worrall, 105–30. Albany: State University of New York Press.

Sekula, A. 1986. "The Body and the Archive." *October* 39 (Winter): 3–64.

Shaw, C. R. 1930. *The Jack Roller*. Chicago: University of Chicago Press.

Shaw, C. R, F. M. Zorbaugh, H. D. McKay, and L. S. Cottre. 1929. *Delinquency Areas*. Chicago: University of Chicago Press.

Shaw, M. 1995. "Conceptualizing Violence by Women." In *Gender and Crime*, ed. R. E. Dobash, R. P. Dobash, and L. Noaks, 115–31. Cardiff: University of Wales Press.

Sheldon, W. H. 1949. *Varieties of Delinquent Youth*. New York: Harper.

Shilling, C. 2003. *The Body and Social Theory*. Thousand Oaks, Calif.: Sage.

Short, J. F. 1982. "Life History, Autobiography, and the Life Cycle." In *The Jack Roller at Seventy*, ed. J. Snodgrass, 135–52. Lexington, Mass.: Lexington Books.

Shover, N. 1996. *Great Pretenders: Pursuits and Careers of Persistent Thieves*. Boulder, Colo.: Westview Press.

Shover, N., and S. Norland. 1978. "Sex Roles and Criminality: Science or Conventional Wisdom?" *Sex Roles* 4 (1): 111–25.

Sutherland, E. H. 1924. *Criminology*. Philadelphia: Lippincott.

———. 1926. "The Biological and Sociological Processes." *Papers and Proceedings of the*

Twentieth Annual Meeting of the American Sociological Society 20: 58–65.

——. 1932. "Social Process in Behavior Problems." *Publications of the American Sociological Society* 26: 55–61.

——. 1937. *The Professional Thief.* Chicago: University of Chicago Press.

——. 1939. *Principles of Criminology.* Philadelphia: Lippincott.

——. 1947. *Principles of Criminology.* Philadelphia: Lippincott.

——. 1956. "Development of the Theory." In *Edwin H. Sutherland: On Analyzing Crime,* ed. K. Schuessler, 13–29. Chicago: University of Chicago Press.

Thomas, W. I., and F. Znaniecki. 1927 (1958). *The Polish Peasant in Europe and America.* New York: Dover.

Thorne, B. 1993. *Gender Play: Girls and Boys in School.* New Brunswick, N.J.: Rutgers University Press.

Thrasher, F. M. 1927. *The Gang: A Study of 1,313 Gangs in Chicago.* Chicago: University of Chicago Press.

Totten, M. 2000. *Guys, Gangs, and Girlfriend Abuse.* Toronto: Broadview Press.

Turner, B. S. 1996. *The Body and Society: Explorations in Social Theory.* 2nd ed. Thousand Oaks, Calif.: Sage.

Walker, R., ed. 1995. *To Be Real: Telling the Truth and Changing the Face of Feminism.* New York: Anchor Books.

Walsh, A. 2002. *Biosocial Criminology: Introduction and Integration.* Cincinnati, Ohio: Anderson.

West, C., and S. Fenstermaker. 1995. "Doing Difference." *Gender and Society* 9 (1): 8–37.

West, C., and D. H. Zimmerman. 1987. "Doing Gender." *Gender and Society* 1 (2): 125–51.

Wikan, U. 1984. "Shame and Honour: A Contestable Pair." *Man* 19: 635–52.

Williams, S., and G. Bendelow. 1998. *The Lived Body: Sociological Themes, Embodied Issues.* New York: Routledge.

Williams, C. L., and E. J. Heikes. 1993. "The Importance of Researcher's Gender in the In-Depth Interview: Evidence from Two Case Studies of Male Nurses." *Gender and Society* 7 (2): 280–91.

Williams, W. C. 1986. *The Spirit and the Flesh: Sexual Diversity in American Indian Culture.* Boston: Beacon Press.

Winlow, S. 2001. *Badfellas: Crime, Tradition and New Masculinities.* New York: Berg.

Witz, A. 2000. "Whose Body Matters? Feminist Sociology and the Corporeal Turn in Sociology and Feminism." *Body and Society* 6 (2): 1–24.

Witz, A., and B. Marshall. 2003. "The Quality of Manhood: Masculinity and Embodiment in the Sociological Tradition." *The Sociological Review* 51 (31): 339–56.

Wright, R. T., and S. Decker. 1994. *Burglars on the Job: Street Life and Residential Break-ins.* Boston: Northeastern University Press.

——. 1997. *Armed Robbers in Action: Stickups and Street Culture.* Boston: Northeastern University Press.

Yancey Martin, P. 2003. "'Said and Done' Versus 'Saying and Doing': Gendering Practices, Practicing Gender at Work." *Gender and Society* 17 (3): 342–66.

Young, A. 1996. *Imagining Crime: Textual Outlaws and Criminal Conversations.* Thousand Oaks, Calif.: Sage.

Young, I. M. 1990. *Throwing Like a Girl and other Essays in Feminist Philosophy and Social Theory.* Bloomington: Indiana University Press.

INDEX

ABOUT THE AUTHOR

James W. Messerschmidt is professor of sociology at the University of Southern Maine. He is the author of numerous books on gender and crime, including *Capitalism, Patriarchy, and Crime*; *Masculinities and Crime*; and *Nine Lives*.